OUTSTRETCHED ARMS OF GRACE

For God so loved the world that he gave his one and only Son, that whoever believes in him shall not perish but have eternal life.

– John 3:16

Other books by Stephen A. Macchia:

OUTSTRETCHED ARMS OF GRACE

A 40-Day
Lenten Devotional

STEPHEN A. MACCHIA

LEADERSHIP
TRANSFORMATIONS INC.
FORMATION | DISCERNMENT | RENEWAL

Published by Leadership Transformations
P.O. Box 338, Lexington, MA 02420
www.leadershiptransformations.org

September 2015
Printed in the United States of America.

Library of Congress Cataloging-in-Publication Data
Macchia, Stephen A., 1956–
Outstretched Arms of Grace / Stephen A. Macchia.
ISBN 978-0692614952 (pbk.)
Religion / Christian Life / Devotional

Dedicated to

Br. David Vryhof and the Society of
Saint John the Evangelist

with gratitude to God for the countless ways they
faithfully and generously offer soul hospitality with
Christlike humility, wisdom, love, and outstretched
arms of grace.

*In this Lenten series you are invited to consider Jesus' "outstretched arms of grace" toward all who followed him as disciples, seeking to emulate his life, self-sacrifice, and humble service to others. Each day we will reflect on one distinct time and way Jesus stretched out his arms of grace to all who **beheld** his glory, **believed** his message, **belonged** as his disciples, and sought to **become** more and more like his image and with more of their true identity in Christ Alone.*

Table of Contents

Introduction

Dear Friend,

The season of Lent is a solemn time in the liturgical calendar that begins on Ash Wednesday and continues for the next six weeks until we approach Easter Sunday. It's a forty day period of time, counting just the Monday-Saturday's, since it's assumed our faith communities will be gathering for worship on Sunday's and provide additional Lenten focus for the soul. The traditional purpose of Lent is for the devout believer to take this time to be single-minded and heartfelt in commemorating the sacrificial suffering of Jesus on the cross. Therefore, the preparation of the soul for Holy Week includes disciplines such as prayer, self-denial, repentance of sins, and generosity. Many Christians today celebrate Lent as a part of their denomination, local church, or small group.

Why forty days? Many times God's people waited forty days or forty years for God's will to be accomplished. In the Old Testament, Moses spent forty days on Mount Sinai with God (Exodus 24:18); Elijah spent forty days and nights walking to Mount Horeb (1 Kings 19:8); Noah and his family were spared

1

in the great flood that lasted forty days and nights (Genesis 7:4); Jonah prophesied of judgment to the city of Ninevah which was forty days in which to repent or be destroyed (Jonah 3:4); and the Hebrew people wandered in the wilderness forty years while traveling to the Promised Land (Numbers 14:33).

Jesus spent forty days in the wilderness, where he both fasted and was tempted by the devil (Matthew 4:1–2, Mark 1:12–13, Luke 4:1–2). He overcame all three of Satan's temptations by citing Scripture to the devil, at which point the devil left him, angels ministered to Jesus, and he began his ministry. Jesus further said that his disciples should fast "when the bridegroom shall be taken from them" (Matthew 9:15), long considered a reference to his Passion. It is also the traditional belief that Jesus lay in the tomb for forty hours before rising from the dead and leaving his grave clothes behind for his followers to discover. With forty days of preparation, Lent has great significance to many historical events in the life of the Church.

Lent comes to its pinnacle during Holy Week, when we remember the death, burial and resurrection of Jesus. During this week we begin on Palm Sunday, when the crowds worshiped him as he entered Jerusalem on the back of a donkey. We witness afresh the meaning of Maundy Thursday, when Jesus instituted the Lord's Supper and humbly washed the feet of his disciples. From there we enter Good Friday, when the crowds have turned against him and demanded his crucifixion. We watch once more the beatings, whippings, anguish, and torment of his accusers, with the penultimate sacrifice of his nail-pierced hands and feet on the cross at Calvary. But, the drama doesn't end there with the darkness of death. We're led to the empty tomb, and into the bright light of joy-filled Resurrection Day.

During Lent many will abstain from some kind of "luxury" such as sweets, or meat, or travel, or any other self-indulgence that keeps one from remembering the awful curse of the cross. Others will add to their lifestyles some additional expression of devotion to Christ, such as a daily reader, additional attendance at worship gatherings, volunteering services to those in need, noticing or emphasizing a particular practice, or joining a group studying a Lenten topic. Still others will choose to become more generous during Lent, sending cards, gifts, and tokens of affection to loved ones, or making financial offerings anonymously to those in need. Whatever you choose, each option is merely an invitation not a requirement. It's perfectly fine to not delete, add, or multiply anything new during this season. What's most important is ensuring your heart is intentionally attentive to the gifts that Jesus has given by way of his ultimate sacrifice on the cross: forgiveness of sins, fullness of life, and a forever home awaiting you in heaven.

What will be your choice this Lenten season, when for forty days we will all join our hearts in united devotion, anticipating once more the celebration of the Risen Christ? May the journey ahead be good for your soul.

Coming alongside you with joy,

Steve Macchia
Founder and President
Leadership Transformations

Day 1: Ash Wednesday

In the Dusty Birthplace

Read: Genesis 3:19 and Luke 2:1-7

Today is Ash Wednesday, when in many Christian churches pilgrims gather to worship and repent of their sins, being reminded once more of their mortality. Typically, there is a time to come forward to have ashes placed on the forehead, often in the sign of the cross. The minister will recite one of two phrases, depending on the denominational setting. "Remember that you are dust, and to dust you shall return" which is taken from Genesis 3:19 on the heels of Adam and Eve's fall to the temptation of the enemy. Another option is "Repent and believe in the Gospel" from Mark 1:14, making explicit (repent and believe) what is implied (own your mortality and acknowledge your need to trust Christ for your salvation) in the first spoken words.

Either way, the words spoken from Scripture upon receiving the ashes are reminders of our mortality, and our corresponding need to repent of our sinfulness and submit to the truths of the Gospel. It's a fitting way to enter Lent, as we usher in a season dedicated to the renewal of our souls. The ashes placed on foreheads are burned from the previous year's palm branches from Palm Sunday worship. As we approach Holy Week and prepare our hearts for Easter, the symbolism of today is poignant.

We fast today in remembrance of our sinful mortality (from ashes to ashes, dust to dust), as we prepare our hearts for the feast of the Gospel of Easter and the hope of resurrection life for all eternity. We fast today in order to embrace the suffering our Lord assumed in our behalf by his immortality, his incarnation, and his infinite love for all.

When we turn to Luke 2, we are reminded of the miraculous and holy birth of our Lord Jesus. Here in the sawdust manger, the immortal One is born into this world as our Savior. Jesus' new place in this world is all a part of God's magnificent plan for our redemption. Because of Jesus' arrival into actual time and space on planet earth, his Advent and Incarnation are gifts we treasure deeply. This dramatic symbol of God's infinite love for his beloved children is representative of his willingness to become familiar with our status as human beings for a season. God became man... the infinite joined the finite...heaven came down to earth...and Jesus showed us the way home to the heart of God.

In the lowly manger, humbly born, Jesus was welcomed with the open arms of love from his mother Mary, father Joseph, and the entire universe now rejoices.

Behold his dusty birthplace as you believe the Gospel once more. Know with certainty that you belong to the family of God, and become today a repentant mortal, fully aware of your sinfulness, and your desperate need for a hope-filled Savior.

Day 2: Thursday

❧

In the Starry Night

Read: Luke 2: 8-20

Entering the Lenten season can be pretty abrupt. In the midst of our normal lives, all of a sudden we're encouraged to press the pause button and hop back on the bus marked "Lent" once more. The sign that says "This way to Easter" catches us off guard and we scramble to know how best to participate in the journey to the cross. We've traveled this way and to the same destination before. The scenery looks pretty similar. So, how do we embrace this year's pilgrimage in a new and soul-refreshing way?

When the shepherds were out in the fields keeping watch over their flocks by night, they were shocked when the bright star was shining that night when Jesus was born. We look back to that occasion as we enter Lent, for it was at that moment when the promise of his coming into the world was fulfilled. In Lent we anticipate his departure from his earthly life and ministry and his return to his eternal home with the Godhead in heaven.

The shepherds' utter surprise at the shining of such a brilliant beacon of light in the midst of their darkness led them into worship. When the glory of the Lord shone around them they were terrified. But, the angels came praising God and saying, "Glory to God in the highest, and on earth peace to them on whom his favor rests." The shepherds response was classic worship: let's go and see...so they hurried and found Jesus...and after seeing Jesus they left ecstatic with their discovery and shared the good news with all who were witnesses of their glorifying and praising God.

Like the humble hearted shepherds who were adorned with the presence of Jesus, so should we long for the same this Lenten season. We know the meta-narrative that awaits us in our journey to Holy Week and Easter. We've traveled this path in previous years and with similar companions. But, what can be different this time: eyes alert to the ways Jesus stretches out his arms for us in our comings and goings. And, when we behold him in our midst, to glorify God and offer fresh testimony to others.

Will you purpose to keep your eyes wide open so you can see Jesus this Lent? He may appear to you in the reading of his Word and the singing of his love in worship, or in the breaking of bread in fellowship with others of like heart and mind, or in your quiet place of alone time in prayer. Jesus may come to you this Lenten season through a warm embrace of a friend, or the kindness of a helpful deed, or even in a difficulty, pain or sorrow when you have only one place to turn.

Behold him in the starry night, believe him in the break of day, belong to him in the fellowship of the saints, and become like him in your worship and witness.

Day 3: Friday

❧

In the Gifts of Life

Read: Matthew 2: 1-12

You might be thinking…why are we reading about the visit of the Magi on our journey to Easter? For one simple reason: to remember and give thanks, and with awe and wonder. We recall with delight the marvelous ways the wise men found their way to Jesus, and being overjoyed with their discovery "bowed down and worshiped him." Then they opened their treasures and presented him with gifts.

In the stillness of the night the wise men followed the star with delight, and what they found brought complete joy to their hearts. Similarly, when all who are seeking Jesus find him, no matter if they are shepherds or magi, business leaders or college educators, homemakers or pastors, their souls are filled up with everlasting love only Jesus can deliver. And, in the midst of the moment, they can't help but offer back to him with outstretched arms the fullness of their lives.

Think about it for a moment…who else brought Jesus extravagant gifts in response to God's outstretched arms of grace extended to earth's inhabitants in the life of Jesus? For the Magi, they knew he was someone extra special, a child sent from heaven "as the king of the Jews" and they did everything possible; even defy King Herod, to be near the baby Jesus when he was born in Bethlehem in Judea, just as the prophet Micah had foretold.

So, imagine the scene for yourself. You are living in the time of King Herod and word comes to you that your king has been born in a manger, under the bright sky of winter. You pack up all your belongings and make sure you have a splendid gift to share with the child and his family. You travel over hill and dale to the place where the Christ child lays freshly newborn, still nursing and finding breath and life in the loving arms of his beloved parents. What is your response in this amazing encounter with the Christ child? Are you still in awe and wonder as you prepare to watch him head now to the cross?

This Lenten season, may I be so bold to encourage you toward spontaneous responses in worship, such as repentance and joy? And, in your interactions with others, to be generous with grace, mercy, forgiveness, and even tangible gifts of love? Each time I consider the waiting and watching of the Magi, followed by their journey to find Jesus, and then their response of gift giving, I'm struck by the contrast with my own life. How much of my life is consumed (or not) by anticipation of Jesus' arrival in the everydayness of my existence? How willing am I to give back to him and others extravagantly, in the manner in which Jesus has given to me?

Behold him with awe... believe in him once more... belong to his tribe with firm resolve... and, become a generous lover, forgiver, and reconciler. May it be so!

Day 4: Saturday

❧

In the Sacred Light

Read: Isaiah 7: 14; 8:8; Matthew 1: 23;
and John 15: 5

Immortal One, born miraculously of a virgin, entering humbly into this world in a manger, worshiped by lowly shepherds, awe-struck in the eyes of wise men, God has indeed joined humankind and lands safely on planet earth. Immanuel, God is with us. Let all the earth rejoice!

The prophet Isaiah foretold his arrival through the sign of the impossible: a virgin will conceive miraculously by the power of the Holy Spirit and a son will be born. Isaiah pronounced the King's arrival by the metaphor of the outspread wings of the floodwaters which will cover the breadth of the land. O Immanuel, the prophet declares, you will cover the earth with outstretched arms of grace.

During Lent we are reminded once more of Immanuel, the God who has, is, and continues to be with us. This Immanuel is Jesus, sent to cover our worlds completely and expansively, enveloping our lives from the inside out. When Jesus begins human life, the God-man reaches out to all who cross his path with a generous earnestness and an intentional proactivity which will be marveled at by some and stiff armed by many others. But to those who receive his gift of love, do so with outstretched arms of anticipation and gladness.

God with us, Immanuel, therefore invites us to a "with God" existence. His presence, power and peace are always being initiated toward us, all the time and in every circumstance. Frankly, our great God, personalized in Jesus, will always come to us in merciful, grace-filled, forgiving, and tender-loving ways. The question is not whether he will deliver on his promises to be with us, instead, will we keep our word of desire and decree that we choose to be with him?

It's a "with God" life that matters most to all who claim his name as Christian. During Lent, we have many opportunities to abide with him as he so graciously abides with us. What does your "with God" existence look like and how is it you wish to show your allegiance to Jesus this Lenten season?

Perhaps you might consider how best to pray during Lent...doing all the talking to God, or choosing instead to notice, listen, and give thanks? Perhaps you might sense an invitation from God to repent of your sinfulness and turn back to godliness? Perhaps you might encourage and celebrate the lives of those who know you best and love you most? Perhaps you might focus more on slowing down and being more, rather than racing faster and accomplishing the most?

Behold him in the sacred light of this new day... believe his promise to be with you forever... belong to his lineage as a faithful disciple... become a person enveloped by his unconditional love. Amen.

First Sunday in Lent

Sunday Readings for Personal Reflection

Sabbath rest is your soul's first priority today. Cease from your work week and find rest in God alone. Worship with your faith community and remember together Jesus' sacrificial life of love. Celebrate your life in Christ and embrace your true identity in Him. As you spend time alone with God in your prayer closet, consider reviewing and prayerfully reflecting upon the following Lenten readings for this Sunday. They are taken from The Revised Common Lectionary (Vanderbilt Divinity Library) and are listed in Years A, B, and C, depending on the "cycle" for this church year. Consult resources from your local church, denomination, or the internet to determine which readings/church year are most appropriate. Or, simply choose one of the groupings below and meditate on the richness of God's Word…I'm sure God will be pleased with your desires no matter what grouping you read.

First Sunday in Lent - Year A

Genesis 2:15-17; 3:1-7

Psalm 32

Romans 5:12-19

Matthew 4:1-11

First Sunday in Lent - Year B

Genesis 9:8-17

Psalm 25:1-10

1 Peter 3:18-22

Mark 1:9-15

First Sunday in Lent - Year C

Deuteronomy 26:1-11

Psalm 91:1-2, 9-16

Romans 10:8b-13

Luke 4:1-13

Day 5: Monday

❧

In the Marketplace

Read: Matthew 13:55, Mark 6:3, and Luke 2:41-52

Today we round the corner from the prophetic word spoken about Jesus' arrival to earth, his subsequent miraculous birth, and enter his childhood story. But, frankly, there isn't much that the biblical text offers us about his youth, beyond a few known facts. We know that he was raised in Nazareth, a very humble community. He had brothers and sisters, and the Bible provides us the names of his brothers, James, Joseph, Simon and Judas.

We also know that when he was twelve he tipped his hand about his unusual wisdom when with his family at the Feast of the Passover in Jerusalem he stayed behind in the temple courts, sitting among the teachers, listening to them and asking them questions. It took his parents three days to find him (the original "home alone" but in this case home in the temple!).

When Joseph and Mary finally found him, his mother asked him, "Son, why have you treated us like this?" Jesus answered them, "Didn't you know I had to be in my Father's house?" His mother treasured these things in her heart.

Jesus was always about his father's business. As a child one can surmise that he joined his father and brothers in Joseph's carpentry business. Joseph undoubtedly would have taught his sons the trade, including Jesus. We don't know for certain what that trade was, but some claim they made wooden plows. We are left to our imagination about how Jesus was in the carpentry shop. Most likely he was a good learner, a diligent worker, a faithful team player. Can you give yourself permission to imagine Jesus in the carpenter's household, among his siblings, working, resting, completing jobs, enjoying meals, and delighting in conversation with those he lived, loved and served?

When as a twelve year old, he was also about his Father's business. His heavenly Father sent him to earth to live among the leaders of the time and to share all that he knew to be true with all who would eventually follow him. Those who heard him interact with the teachers in the temple courts were amazed at his understanding and answers. When his parents finally found him they were astonished.

In both the carpenter's shop and the temple courts,

Jesus lived comfortably in the marketplace of wood carving and truthful ideas. He was a listener, a learner, and a dispenser of truth every place he traveled. His outstretched arms of grace began to emerge early on. His arms of love would continue to be held wide open to all who would receive his message. On the job, no matter the setting, he remained faithful.

Behold him in the marketplace as the carpenter's son and the dispenser of truth. Believe once more the incarnational story of Jesus living in a human family, with earthly parents and siblings. Belong to the incredible storyline which invites a deeper trust. Become a sincerely devoted recipient of truth today.

Day 6: Tuesday

❧

In the River

Read: Luke 3:21-23

When others were being baptized in the Jordan River, the thirty-year-old Jesus was also coming to be baptized. This was yet another powerful example of his outstretched arms of grace. Here, Jesus willingly joins the larger group of those coming to the waters of baptism and submits his heart into the hands of the baptizer, and ultimately into the loving hands of God.

As he was praying, heaven was opened and the Holy Spirit descended on him in bodily form like a dove. And a voice came from heaven, "You are my Son, whom I love, with you I am well pleased."

The Triune God – Father, Son and Holy Spirit – in unity of purpose and love, each fulfilling unique but completely integrated purposes with one another. The Spirit appears in the form of a dove, a tangible expression of the significance of this event for the Son of God and all who would witness this event. The Father gives voice to his affection for Jesus, clearly announced from heaven for all to hear. Three key messages emerge in this grand sentiment: first of all, Jesus' relationship with the Father as his Son; secondly, a declarative pronouncement of love; and thirdly, an affirmation of delightfully great pleasure.

The mission and ministry of Jesus is officially coming to fruition. His younger years with his family and among his community were preparing for this event and his forthcoming service to others. Here in the waters of baptism God is announcing from heaven that Jesus is now moving intentionally into relationships, worship and service, all of which will declare the Kingdom of heaven. This was a defining moment, an inflection point for Jesus, which would eventually be looked back upon as significant.

By far, the high point of his baptism is the Father's declaration of his belovedness as a son. This status was of central importance to all who would eventually call upon him as Savior and Lord. His beloved place in the wide-open arms of the Father would be a continual reflection from Jesus to all who cross his path. Gracious, unconditional love would become the centerpiece of his message, his mission, and his ministry moving forward to the cross.

Can you recognize today how dearly God loves you

as his child? Can you acknowledge the outstretched arms of grace extended to you each moment of the day? Can you recall the many ways the love of Jesus has been your mainstay, the music in your ears, and the meaning of your with God life? Can you point out to others the outstretched loving arms of grace, mercy, forgiveness, joy and love offered by Jesus?

Behold Jesus in the river of gladness and salvation; believe the Gospel of unconditional love; belong today to the family of God who are being loved into the Kingdom; and become so filled up with love that you can't help but freely and generously share Jesus' love with all who will cross your path even today.

Day 7: Wednesday

❧

In the Wilderness

Read: Luke 4: 1-13

Jesus, full of the Holy Spirit, and on the heels of his spectacular baptism, was led by the same Spirit into the desert, where for forty days he was tempted by the devil. This is the account that defines for us the true meaning of Lent. These forty days for our Lord of fasting and temptation were defining and confirming days for his love of his Father, the Word of God, and the Kingdom he represented. Those very same declarations are what we ascribe as well in our Lenten fast this time around.

Each time Jesus was tempted by the devil, he responded with the strength of the Word of God. Tempting his appetites, by urging him to tell stone to become bread, Jesus responds, "Man does not live on bread alone." Tempting his authority, by offering him all the kingdoms of this world, Jesus replies, "Worship the Lord your God and serve him daily." Tempting his abilities, by suggesting he throw himself down from the highest point of the temple, Jesus retorts, "Do not put the Lord your God to the test." Each rejoinder was quoted from the book of Deuteronomy, the Law that was on the heart of Jesus.

It's remarkable to consider the immediate challenge given to Jesus after the joyful experience of his baptism. From heaven's declarative of love and affection, to earth's most difficult trials and tribulations. To be given over to the devil's schemes in the middle of the wilderness, showed all who would learn of this drama how Jesus was tempted as we are too. And yet, unlike us, he exits those forty days unscathed and never succumbs to any of the luring temptations offered to him. His willingness to enter this season of temptation is another very poignant example of Jesus' outstretched arms of grace toward all who would eventually listen to his voice, obey his call, and follow his example.

All of us understand the enticement of temptation, because we've all faced our fair share of allurement. Each time we are tempted to walk away from God and toward sin, we are brought face to face with our basic human condition. In the dark corners of such trials we are confronted by a much deeper choice of the will. It's only in the light of God's Word, and the enlightenment of God's Spirit, that we will have the prayerful courage to say no in order to say yes to Jesus' invitation to walk his way.

What temptations are standing in your way most consistently? What are the vulnerable places in your life that the enemy of your soul knows best to torment? How will you lean on God and your spiritual friends to defend you from such anguish? Will you trust Jesus to stand in the gap and keep you from falling prey to such temptations even today?

Behold him in the wilderness confronting the devil's enticement; believe Jesus to strengthen you to say no to any temptation; belong firmly to the family of the empowered; and become steadfast in your soul.

Day 8: Thursday

❧

In the Synagogue

Read: Luke 4: 14-21 and Matthew 25: 31-46

After being released from the wilderness experience of successfully rejecting the devil's temptations, Jesus returns to his hometown Nazareth. On the Sabbath he enters the synagogue, as was his custom, and he stood up to read from the prophet Isaiah, "The Spirit of the Lord is on me, because he has anointed me to preach good news to the poor. He has sent me to proclaim freedom for the prisoners and recovery of sight for the blind, to release the oppressed, to proclaim the year of the Lord's favor."

After his baptism in the Jordan, clearly declared the beloved Son of God from heaven, and being consecrated for sacrificial service in the desert, Jesus reenters the synagogue with a renewed holy confidence. Even though in his hometown he was not valued as anything more than Joseph the carpenter's son, he was now validated as the fulfillment of a word spoken long before his earthly arrival. And on that day the prophetic word spoken by Isaiah so long before came to fulfillment in Jesus.

Jesus' mission statement expresses his call to preach good news, proclaiming freedom, recovery, and release to those in bondage to poverty, prison, blindness and oppression. Those who were witnesses of his presence and power would see this made manifest in his life, witness and service to all who will henceforth cross his path. That's exactly what Jesus does for a three-year period, with his arms outstretched in grace. As his disciples see this with their own eyes, Jesus instructs them to do likewise.

By the time he was nearing the end of his earthly ministry, just prior to when he would be handed over to be crucified, Jesus reminds his disciples of their mission statement in the analogy of the separation of the sheep and the goats. The King will call those righteous who feed the hungry, give drink to the thirsty, shelter to the homeless, clothing to the poor, healing to the sick, and liberty to those who are in prison. To all who do not heed this mission will be called goats, and they will be sent away to eternal punishment. But, to the righteous who do as Jesus suggest, they will experience eternal life.

This concise summary of mission is a great starting point for all healthy disciples who long to be in the center of God's will. To offer the gospel of freedom and joy in Jesus is to invite another to belong to Jesus and in doing so to listen attentively to his voice and live abundantly for his glory. During Lent we will have many opportunities to offer our own outstretched arms of love to others in need of a cup of cold water in Jesus' name. We will come across the hungry, the hurting, and the homeless, and we'll be faced with the opportunity to offer healing in Jesus' name. What will you choose?

Behold Jesus in the synagogue as he proclaims his mission; believe firmly in the truth that sets us free; belong to those who pursue Kingdom values; and become a loving disciple with holy determination.

Day 9: Friday

❦

In the Homestead

Read: Luke 10:38-42 and John 11: 1-37; 12: 1-3

Jesus not only had disciples with whom he had close relationships, but he also developed deep friendships, especially with a family from Bethany. Two were sisters, Mary and Martha, and the other was their brother Lazarus. The encounters with this family were deeply significant to Jesus and very meaningful to the three siblings. In fact, so important that we find him in their home during times when each would experience the fullness of his presence, power and peace.

The Gospels record for us a small handful of such encounters. On one such visit Jesus is reminding Martha that even though she has the gift of hospitality, there are times when such worrying and scurrying about can distract one from spiritual receptivity. He points to Mary her sister, who took time for uninterrupted listening and pondering at his feet. Instead of being upset about many things, only one thing is needed: attentiveness to the voice of Jesus.

On another occasion, Mary and Martha are searching for Jesus to heal their brother Lazarus. His sickness had overcome him to the point of death. They believed that Jesus could restore him from his sickness, but didn't fully realize he could also raise him from the dead. When Jesus finally makes it to their home, Lazarus has died. Jesus weeps. He loved Lazarus and was sad that he had died. So, he prayed to his Father in heaven, and asked them to roll away the stone where Lazarus had been buried for four days. And, for the glory of God to be released in their presence, Lazarus was raised from the dead.

"I am the resurrection and the life. He who believes in me will live, even though he dies; and whoever lives and believes in me will never die." These words came true in their incredible encounter with Jesus who powerfully demonstrated the truth of God's Word in raising Lazarus from the dead. The peace that filled their souls from this fresh encounter with Jesus deepened their affection as friends and devoted followers of God.

Later we see Mary taking a pint of pure nard, an expensive perfume, pouring it on Jesus' feet, wiping his feet with her hair. The house was filled with the fragrance of the perfume. The presence of the Spirit of God rested on that household as together they prepared for Jesus' final days on earth. The perfume had been saved for his burial, an offering of their devotion to Christ.

You too are a friend of Jesus. You too can offer your finest fragrance of love for his glory during Lent.

Behold him in the homestead of his dearly loved friends; believe in his power to perform a miracle of grace and healing in your midst; belong to those who pursue his daily companionship; and become a disciple who knows that only one thing matters: unhurried friendship with Jesus now and for all eternity.

Day 10: Saturday

❧

In the Set Apart Place

Read: Mark 1: 35-39; 6:45-56 and Luke 5:16

Jesus often withdrew to lonely, solitary places and prayed.

In the first chapter of Mark, we are reminded of Jesus' ministry throughout Galilee. He proclaims the good news of God, and calls the first of his disciples. "Come, follow me and I will make you fishers of men" he pronounces to Peter and Andrew, James and John, all who were fishermen by trade were now fishermen by ministry. He goes on to Capernaum, teaching in the synagogue, driving an evil spirit out of the man who was violently distraught and sets him free. He heals Simon's mother in-law and many others who were sick and demon-possessed. More and more examples of his outstretched arms of grace.

But, very early in the morning, while it was still dark, Jesus got up, left the house and went off to a solitary place, where he prayed. When the disciples found him, they urged him to return to the towns they had served the day prior, but Jesus leads them instead into nearby villages to share the good news.

In the second incident, after the feeding the five thousand, Jesus sends his disciples across the lake ahead of him to Bethsaida, while he dismisses the crowd. Immediately thereafter, Jesus leaves them all and went into the hills to pray. Since the disciples didn't really understand what had transpired in the miracle of the loaves and fish, their hearts were hardened. So, when Jesus is coming alongside them walking on water while the wind was howling and they were straining their oars, he had to reassure them of his presence amidst their terror. "Take courage! It is I. Don't be afraid." When he climbed into the boat the wind died down and the disciples were completely amazed.

Do you notice the contrast between the calm, peace-filled Jesus and the anxious, fearful disciples? In the first story the disciples are ecstatic with what they had witnessed, and they wanted to see it all again. On the lake, they were frightened by both the wind storm and the ghost they thought was walking on the water, who was actually Jesus. From ecstasy to fearfulness...the inclination of the disciples was diametrically opposite of Jesus, who was consistently centered, focused, and peaceful.

If it was Jesus' regular priority to distance himself from the crowds, disappear from the noise and confusion of his surroundings, in order to pray... how much more we should consider the same. We live in a loud, busy, complex world, and our lives mirror our culture in so many ways. If we never find a healthy distance or create life-giving boundaries from the cacophony of this world, we will never hear the symphony God longs to play for us in our hearts and souls. Choose today a solitary place and pray.

Behold Jesus in a solitary place; believe in the same priority for your own soul; belong to those who long for his deep companionship; become that child of God who longs for ever more time alone with Jesus.

Second Sunday in Lent

Sunday Readings for Personal Reflection

Sabbath rest is your soul's first priority today. Cease from your work week and find rest in God alone. Worship with your faith community and remember together Jesus' sacrificial life of love. Celebrate your life in Christ and embrace your true identity in Him. As you spend time alone with God in your prayer closet, consider reviewing and prayerfully reflecting upon the following Lenten readings for this Sunday. They are taken from The Revised Common Lectionary (Vanderbilt Divinity Library) and are listed in Years A, B, and C, depending on the "cycle" for this church year. Consult resources from your local church, denomination, or the worldwide web to determine which readings/church year are most appropriate. Or, simply choose one of the groupings below and meditate on the richness of God's Word...I'm sure God will be pleased with your desires no matter what grouping you read.

Second Sunday in Lent - Year A

> Genesis 12:1-4a
> Psalm 121
> Romans 4:1-5, 13-17
> John 3:1-17 *or Matthew 17:1-9*

Second Sunday in Lent - Year B

> Genesis 17:1-7, 15-16
> Psalm 22:23-31
> Romans 4:13-25
> Mark 8:31-38 *or Mark 9:2-9*

Second Sunday in Lent - Year C

> Genesis 15:1-12, 17-18
> Psalm 27
> Philippians 3:17-4:1
> Luke 13:31-35 *or Luke 9:28-36, (37-43a)*

Day 11: Monday

Giving Disciples Invitation

Read: Matthew 4: 18-22 and Luke 5: 1-11

As Jesus was walking along the shoreline of the Sea of Galilee, he points out two brothers who were fishermen. He calls out a simple invitation, "Come, follow me, and I will make you fishers of men." At first we read this and are astonished how quickly the men responded. In fact, the Scriptures use the words "at once" and "without delay" and "immediately." Upon reflection, you might wonder, "Who in their right mind would drop their nets and blindly follow the voice of a stranger?"

Thankfully, Luke gives us a bit more detail in his rendering of the story; they weren't so blind after all. Jesus was indeed standing by the lake, with people starting to crowd around him and listening to him share the Word of God. So, as the crowd was thickening, he noticed two boats left there by the fishermen. One of them belonged to Simon (Peter) so he asked if it would be ok if he got in and if Simon would take him out away from the shore so Jesus could continue to teach the crowd of listeners.

In return for his gratitude, and after he was finished speaking, Jesus offers his outstretched arms of love to Simon by suggesting that he row out to the deep water and let the nets down for a catch. Simon respectfully shares with Jesus that they were hard at work all night long but hadn't caught anything. However, Simon and his companions eventually do as Jesus suggested, and they catch more fish than their nets could handle. In fact, so many fish that their boats began to sink. They were astonished, so Simon falls down at Jesus' feet and pleads with him to "Go away from me, Lord; I am a sinful man!"

Jesus comforts Simon Peter with the simple response, "Don't be afraid; from now on you will catch men." It was at that moment that Peter, his brother Andrew, James and his brother John, left everything behind and followed Jesus.

There is something very heartening in this story of invitation and followership. It's all about Jesus' love for others, his demonstration of that love through acts of kindness and miraculous affection. Each time he revealed himself and invited others to follow him, it was in the context of their normal lives and relationships. Jesus comes alongside others in very personal ways, reveals himself in ordinary and extraordinary ways, and then makes an offer few could refuse.

In the same way Jesus has come beside you, knows your name, is sensitive to your context, and desirous of expressing his love in tangible and intangible ways.

Behold him giving his disciples a loving invitation to follow; believe he will keep calling out your name; belong to the companions of Jesus who love to follow him; and become fully alive in the prospect of eternal invitations which will lead you into an abundant life in Christ.

Day 12: Tuesday

Giving Disciples Instruction

Read: Matthew 10: 1-20

When Jesus called his disciples to follow him, he also gave them authority to drive out evil spirits and to heal every disease and sickness. It's amazing to consider the responsibility assigned to the twelve men he chose to be his closest companions. The fact that he empowered them to act in his behalf, giving them full power to do as he would do if he were in their sandals, dramatically displays his generously outstretched arms of grace.

As he sent them out to serve in his name, he offered them some very specific instructions. They were to go to the lost sheep of Israel, with an intentionality that defined them as emissaries of Jesus. As they traveled along their assigned pathway of service, they were given a specific message: preach the Kingdom of heaven is near. The Kingdom was Jesus' favorite topic; he spoke of this more than any other issue. His desire was for his disciples to embrace and embody the richness of Christ's Kingdom.

The disciples' ministry was to heal the sick, raise the dead, cleanse the leper, and drive out demons. They were set apart to perform miraculous healing in Jesus' name, so that God would receive all the glory, honor and praise. They were not to be entrapped by anything that would hinder their mission, message or ministry. Instead, they were to travel light: no gold, silver or copper in their belts; no bag or extra tunic, sandals or staff for them to carry.

The entirety of Matthew chapter ten is filled with instructions. "Freely they have received, so freely they are to give" was their lived refrain. "He who receives you receives me, and he who receives me receives the one who sent me" (Matthew 10: 40). The disciples would be receivable to others, not because of who they were as remarkable human beings, but as a reflection of the God who sent them out in his name.

Each of us as 21st Century disciples follow the same instruction manual as the 1st Century disciples. The specifics may be edited per generation, but the overarching and guiding principles are cross-generational. We are to travel light. We are to find others who will bless and send us from place to place, as companions who share our faith community and mission. We have a message to proclaim and a ministry to perform...empowered by the Spirit, all for the glory of God, and all for the fulfillment of Christ's Kingdom here on earth. What Kingdom building activity is God calling you to this day? And, more abundantly in this season of your life in Christ?

Behold the King who offers clear instruction to all who follow him; believe in this great God who will make his way clear for you too; belong to the company of disciples who walk with him each new day; and become a faithful disciple who delights to follow Jesus into both familiar and uncharted terrain.

Day 13: Wednesday

Giving Disciples Inclusion

Read: Matthew 10: 16-42

When the disciples were sent out by Jesus, they had no idea how radical would be their message or their Messenger. As Jesus prepares them to spread out and serve side by side, he speaks provocatively and proactively to them. One can only imagine the surprise look on their faces when Jesus makes it clear: they would be sent out like sheep among wolves. Therefore, Jesus urges them to be as shrewd as snakes and as innocent as doves. They were to be on guard against men, for brother will betray brother; father his child; children will rebel against their parents. In fact, Jesus says, all men will hate you because of Me. Following Jesus as 1st Century disciples was filled with suffering, challenge, and hardship, as well as all the miraculous healings, releases from bondage, and abundance of spiritual vitality in Christ.

This is not the kind of message disciples of Jesus in the 21st Century like to hear. We prefer hearing that following Jesus will take us into lands filled with milk and honey, where we will prosper in worldly ways in order to fulfill the dreams we've been taught from childhood to pursue: upward mobility in education, wealth, influence and possessions. But, when we look carefully at the biblical Gospel accounts, we don't see anything like that whatsoever. In fact, quite the contrary. Jesus makes it clear, "Anyone who does not take his cross and follow me is not worthy of me. Whoever finds his life will lose it, and whoever loses his life for my sake will find it."

The Gospel of Jesus requires our full selves in full obedience being fully sold out to fully extend ourselves, so that the message is richly proclaimed in both word and deed. God is love, and when we receive his love the discipleship we're invited into is a whole life devoting our entire life to give our complete life away...to Jesus, for Jesus, and all because of Jesus.

Jesus' outstretched arms of love were opened fully for his disciples to receive. Their lives were transformed from the moment they met Jesus, and their desire to follow him was enhanced over time as they saw him in action. But, living with and for Jesus required each of them to give all of themselves. No turning back. Nothing withheld. No holds barred. No compromise. No love for another more than Jesus. No other life was theirs to live but the one Jesus offered and empowered.

What about you, friend? Freely you've received, will you now freely give? His arms are outstretched toward you; will you welcome the loving embrace of Jesus? Will you give all for the sake of the cross of Christ, the very destination we're heading toward this Lenten season?

Behold Jesus giving his disciples immersion training in discipleship; believe that life and ministry in Jesus is always worth the cost; belong to the fellowship of the suffering; and become a disciple committed to living wholly for Jesus.

Day 14: Thursday

Giving Disciples
Immersion

Read: John 17

The disciples knew that Jesus loved them, from the moment they were invited into the inner circle as followers and friends, all throughout their years together, and most especially as the time drew near for Jesus to leave them and return to his Father in heaven. His "farewell discourse" recorded for us in John 14-17 reveals so much of Jesus' affection for his disciples. All of these words were spoken on the heels of his demonstration of the "fullest extent of his love" for them by washing their feet.

He urges them not to let their hearts become troubled, but to trust in God. He prepares them for his departure, sharing that he is the way and the truth and the life, the only way to the Father. He promises to send them "another Counselor" who will be with them forever, the Holy Spirit of truth and love. He reminds them they are his friends, and promises them that their grief will turn to joy when he's gone.

As he is concluding these remarks, he turns to the Father in prayer. In John 17, Jesus is praying for his own relationship with the Father, noting that he came to earth to complete the work of glorifying the Father throughout the world. Then, he prays for his immediate disciples, for the Father to protect them by the power of his name, so that they may be one. He also prays that his disciples would have the full measure of Jesus' joy within them. And, that the Father would sanctify them by the truth of the Word.

What follows in verses 20-26 is Jesus' prayer for those who would follow him in future generations, including our own. For those he prays for God's glory to be revealed and released through their unity and oneness, "I in them and you in me. May they be brought to complete unity to let the world know that you sent me and have loved them even as you have loved me." The focus of Jesus' heart prayer for disciples of every generation is complete unity, without which the world will never know why Jesus was sent by the Father to earth as the greatest of all expressions of love.

In Jesus' great high priestly prayer of John 17, his outstretched arms of grace embrace us all. No disciple of any millennia since the time of Christ is excluded. In this prayer, Jesus and his Father, along with the Spirit, are praying for all who follow him and claim his name as believers. As we are united as one in Christ, we reveal the glory of God in this watching and waiting, often wounded and skeptical, world. Only as we are one will the world fully know the gospel of peace, joy and love.

Will you join Jesus in fulfilling his prayerful longing for our generation? Will you participate in building unity among all who call themselves Christian?

Behold Jesus blessing his disciples in their community oneness; believe in the priority of unity today; belong to those who choose to be reconcilers and peace makers; become a Christ-follower who desires to see God's glory revealed and released even today.

Day 15: Friday

Giving Disciples Ministry

Read: Mark 6: 30-44

Participating in meaningful ministry was Jesus' goal for his disciples. Not just hanging out with him, traveling throughout Galilee, Judea and Jerusalem, walking, eating, sleeping and doing life together. Instead, the disciples were actively engaged in serving others with and for Jesus.

In this account of the feeding of the five thousand, we see a handful of ways Jesus involves his disciples in serving the needs of others. They first of all reported to Jesus all they had done and taught, keeping close accountability with the Lord. They also joined Jesus in a quiet place where they could rest and be replenished for the days ahead. Jesus invited them to come with him into those solitary places, knowing their need for regular breaks from the crowds that were beginning to exponentially form around Jesus.

On this particular occasion, Jesus had compassion on the large crowd, seeing them as sheep without a shepherd. His teaching ministry was continuing to expand, often late into the evening, in both the countryside and the villages. Seeing their need for food, he instructed his disciples to give them something to eat. They asked, "With just five loaves and two fish?" As the disciples assembled the crowd into groups of hundreds and fifties, he took the loaves and fish and lifted them up to heaven. He gave thanks and broke the loaves, giving the pieces to the disciples to distribute among them all.

After everyone was miraculously fed, the disciples picked up the broken pieces left behind, filling twelve basketfuls of bread and fish. A total of 5,000 were fed on that day. This encounter was enticing each of the disciples to the mission of their Lord Jesus. This inevitably impressed upon their hearts the transformational values of listening, obedience, and faithful service to others in need.

Who among us doesn't want to be engaged in meaningful work for the Kingdom of God? When we know that our efforts are not extended in vain, we share more fully in the mission of God. Every effort in this most miraculous feeding was laced with the compassion of Jesus. Every ounce of energy was expended for the Gospel King Jesus was proclaiming. These experiences solidified the disciples' commitment to more fully participate in Kingdom efforts, with Jesus and as a team.

Whether in the form of miracles, or simple acts of kindness, Jesus offers his disciples meaningful ministry that would expand the swath of the Gospel everywhere they traveled. The grace-filled Gospel was shared freely and generously as a tangible expression of Jesus' outstretched arms of love.

Therefore, behold Jesus inviting his disciples into fruitful ministry; believe firmly in the Gospel that proclaims truth, grace and love both far and wide; belong to the communion of saints who carry on his legacy of love; and become more outward in your service to the King and his Kingdom.

Day 16: Saturday

Giving Disciples Mission

Read: Matthew 10: 6-8; 16: 24-25; 25: 34-40; 28: 18-20

Beginning with his incarnation, Jesus was very clear about his mission. His coming was to serve, not to be served, and to give his life as a ransom for many. He came to be the Good Shepherd who would eternally give his life for his sheep. And, returning from the 40-day wilderness trial, he entered the sanctuary and opened the scroll to announce the fulfillment of the prophetic word of Isaiah. He is the Messiah, anointed by the Spirit to proclaim good news to the poor, proclaim liberty to the prisoners, recovery of sight for the blind, set the oppressed free, and proclaim the year of the Lord's favor.

The gospel of Matthew is loaded with passages that invite Jesus' disciples to embrace his mission to this world. His days on earth were crammed with multiple ways of living that mission, demonstrating it to a watching world, as well as instructing and empowering his disciples to embrace it for themselves. The mission of Jesus was to become the mission of his disciples. As they were sent to the lost sheep of Israel, they were urged to proclaim one central message, "The kingdom of heaven has come near" in Jesus.

Jesus asked his disciples to deny themselves, take up their cross, and follow him. Such a following would include the same kind of ministry Jesus modeled before them. This included feeding the hungry and thirsty, practicing hospitality to the stranger, clothing the naked, looking after the sick, visiting the prisoner, freeing the oppressed, and driving out demons. Since they had freely received such tender mercy and salvation from God, they were to freely give that kind of ministry away to others.

With open, outstretched arms of grace, Jesus held important commandments out before them, beginning with the first and greatest: to love God with heart, soul, mind and strength. The second greatest: to love their neighbor as themselves. And, the ongoing commission for them to go and make disciples of every nation, baptizing them and teaching them to obey all of Jesus' life-transforming principles.

It's fascinating to note that the mission of Jesus is always to the outcast, the oppressed, and the overlooked in society. He passed on this legacy to his disciples then and now. What Jesus desired of his followers was for them to be so filled up with the heart and mind and life of God that they would "overflow" such loveable righteousness and devoted faithfulness to all who would cross their path. Will you say yes to that same invitation today?

Behold Jesus fulfilling his promised mission and inviting his disciples to do the same; believe in the importance of reaching out lovingly to the poor, the prisoner, the blind, and the oppressed; belong to the lineage of faithful Christ-followers who deny themselves for the sake of others; and become a disciple who is so filled up with the ways of God that you indiscriminately overflow his grace to all.

Third Sunday in Lent

Sunday Readings for Personal Reflection

Sabbath rest is your soul's first priority today. Cease from your work week and find rest in God alone. Worship with your faith community and remember together Jesus' sacrificial life of love. Celebrate your life in Christ and embrace your true identity in Him. As you spend time alone with God in your prayer closet, consider reviewing and prayerfully reflecting upon the following Lenten readings for this Sunday. They are taken from The Revised Common Lectionary (Vanderbilt Divinity Library) and are listed in Years A, B, and C, depending on the "cycle" for this church year. Consult resources from your local church, denomination, or the worldwide web to determine which readings/church year are most appropriate. Or, simply choose one of the groupings below and meditate on the richness of God's Word...I'm sure God will be pleased with your desires no matter what grouping you read.

Third Sunday in Lent - Year A

Exodus 17:1-7

Psalm 95

Romans 5:1-11

John 4:5-42

Third Sunday in Lent - Year B

Exodus 20:1-17

Psalm 19

1 Corinthians 1:18-25

John 2:13-22

Third Sunday in Lent - Year C

Isaiah 55:1-9

Psalm 63:1-8

1 Corinthians 10:1-13

Luke 13:1-9

Day 17: Monday

❧

The Sower

Read: Luke 8: 1-15

Jesus often taught in parables, simple and memorable stories with heartfelt and eternal significance. They were offered to his disciples and followers in earshot of his teaching with an earnest desire for their soul's welfare here on earth and for all eternity. They were gifts of Jesus, yet another form of his outstretched arms of grace, for all who were invited to consider the Kingdom of God both present in Christ in the here and now, and yet to come as we await the ultimate summons to heaven.

The parable of the sower is a story about a farmer who plentifully and extravagantly sowed seed indiscriminately on all soils within his reach. Some of the seed fell along an open pathway, where it was trampled upon by passersby and plucked off by birds of the air that flew in to consume it. Some of the seed was strewn upon rocky soil, so that when it birthed any form of life from within the crevices of rock it came up but soon withered, void of much needed moisture. Still other seed was cast among thorns and thistles along the ground, which awaited any form of growth to then squelch and choke to death.

But, some of the seed actually fell along very good soil. These seeds were welcomed by the rich humus of life-giving nutrition. The good soil was well prepared for the seeds arrival, with plenty of moisture to go around, no rocks or weeds in the way of growth, and ample space to be received and effectuated for life. To the seeds, this was a place of absolute delight.

This parable is all about the soil's receptivity of the seed, strewn generously by the Sower. What Jesus is reminding his hearers about is the openness (or lack thereof) of hearts prepared to receive the gospel of the Kingdom of heaven. Jesus himself, the living Word, has been presented without judgment to the entirety of the world. But, the world he blessed with his presence is filled with disparate forms of receptivity about his coming. Many (soils) would reject his love; some (good soil) would receive him.

Along the path: hearts are stolen by the devil; on the rocks: not much room for his abiding presence; in the weeds: worrisome, pursuing riches and pleasures instead of God; but in good soil: noble hearts, persevering and fruitful. With what soil does your soul most resonate today? Are you being stomped upon by the enemy of your soul, or not leaving much space for Jesus to penetrate the recesses of your soul, or are the enticements of this world so all-consuming that you have forgotten to prioritize Jesus?

May the soil of your soul be filled up with the seed of the Sower, so that by receiving the fullness of his outstretched arms of love you are changed from the inside out. Behold his presence; believe his Word; belong to his Kingdom; and become his "junior sower" seeding your world with the grace of Jesus.

Day 18: Tuesday

❧

The Good Samaritan

Read: Luke 10: 25-37

The Parable of the Good Samaritan is follow-up to a conversation Jesus was having with an "expert" of the law, one of those leader types who were know-it-alls during the time of Christ. The "expert" is asking Jesus to defend two questions: What must I do to inherit eternal life? And, who is my neighbor? The first question is about the message of Jesus and the second probes the mission and ministry of Jesus.

To the first question, Jesus replies by affirming the "experts" own answer to the question by his stating the greatest and second greatest commandments, "Love the Lord your God with all your heart and with all your soul and with all your strength and with all your mind; and 'Love your neighbor as yourself.'" But, to the second question, Jesus backs him up against a wall of conviction with his parable.

The parable is pretty simple. It's about a man who was going down from Jerusalem to Jericho when he is stopped in his tracks by a band of robbers. They strip him of his clothing, beat him, and then leave him half dead in the middle of the road. Then, there are three individuals who come upon the stricken man in the road and are confronted with a choice: do I help him or leave him to die? First, a priest happens upon him, but he passes by and walks around on the other side of the road. Secondly, a Levite comes toward him, and after seeing him lying in the road, also passes him on the opposite side of the road.

A third traveler, this time a Samaritan (often hated by the Jews, who would bristle at one being portrayed in a positive light), comes upon the man and took pity on him. He bandages his wounds, puts him on his donkey, takes him to an inn, pays for his care, leaves him in good hands, and even follows up on his needs during his return trip home. So, when Jesus asks the know-it-all to acknowledge which character in the story most depicts a loving neighbor, he's forced to answer "the one who had mercy."

Mercy is the big idea in this parable. Jesus is filled with mercy. The Samaritan is filled with mercy. All who love the Lord with heart, soul, strength and mind are to be filled with mercy toward their neighbor. Jesus' outstretched arms of love are demonstrated through the gift of mercy. Mercy's best descriptors are compassion, kindness, forgiveness, forbearance, favor, charity and blessing. Mercy is most extended toward those who don't deserve it, but who are in desperate need of it. To be merciful is to be willing to extend an embrace of love even when it's inconvenient to do so.

To love God is to love mercy. For when we were most desperate we received mercy.

Behold God's merciful kindness; believe the transformational gospel of mercy; belong to those who are willing to be inconvenienced for the sake of mercy; and become a Jesus-follower who's a repository of mercy.

Day 19: Wednesday

❦

The House
on the Rock

Read: Matthew 7: 24-29

This parable comes after Jesus has so eloquently delivered the magnificent Sermon on the Mount, which included the Beatitudes, and teachings on subjects such as being salt and light, fulfilling the law by practicing the commandments against murder, adultery, divorce, as well as reminders about how to love our enemies, give to the needy, fasting, praying, and not storing up treasures, worrying, or judging others. The parable of the house on the rock is the PS provided by Jesus, which wraps up his prior teachings with an admonition to remain firmly planted on the solid ground of faithfulness.

It's a very straight forward parable: everyone who has heard Jesus' teaching and puts these into practice is like a wise man who built his house on a rock solid foundation. When the inevitable rain comes down and the streams of water rise and the winds blow and beat mercilessly against the sides of the house, it withstands the bad weather without a problem. However, for those who have heard Jesus' teaching and choose not to put them into practice, are like a foolish person, who builds his house on a flimsy, sandy foundation. When the rains come, streams rise, winds blow and beat against the house, the house falls with a great crash. This story and all previous and subsequent teachings of Jesus amazed the crowds.

Did their amazement at the profundity of Jesus' teaching lead them toward a faithful response? The crowds were drop-jawed with awe in his presence, especially the beauty of the Mount of Beatitudes, overlooking the Sea of Galilee. However, their mountain top experience would be short lived, even though many would subsequently be healed of their diseases and released of their captivities. They would follow him for many more miles, as Jesus continually opened his outstretched arms of grace toward them. But, we also know the "rest of the story" - they would ultimately abandon to a tortuous death the very Teacher who introduced to them the abundance of life with God.

Wisdom or foolishness, that is their clear choice. Wisdom is the ability to judge a situation correctly by gathering information and understanding, and then to follow through with appropriate action. It's more than simply following the rules; it's instead the creation of a pathway that leads to the fullness of life. The way of wisdom directs one toward the teachings and corresponding lifestyle choices that honor and please God. For Jesus, he was able to summarize so much of God's teachings in this powerful Sermon on the Mount. This sermon was delivered with outstretched arms of grace.

What is your response to the invitation of Jesus to walk the pathway of wisdom, as opposed to making foolish decisions that lead you off course? You may wish to ponder anew the Sermon on the Mount.

Behold Jesus the Teacher; believe the Truth he wisely presents; belong to those who are amazed at his wisdom; and become wise in your Jesus foundation and in the pathway you are following him today.

Day 20: Thursday

❧

The Prodigal Son

Read: Luke 15: 11-32

Once described as the" forever parable" because it never runs out of deep meaning, the parable of the lost son is filled with eternal significance. The story is about a man who had two sons. The younger son came to the father requesting his share of the estate. So the father divided his property between them. The younger son took off for a distant land, where he squandered his full inheritance on wild living. When a severe famine came to that country he began to be in need. So, he hired himself out to a person who sent him to feed pigs. His stomach was aching for food, and he became desperate.

When he came to his senses, he realized the stupidity of his ways. He set out to go back home to his father and admit his sin, relinquish his status as his son, and offer himself as one of his dad's hired hands.

But, while he was still a long way from home, his father saw him on route and because he was filled with compassion he ran to his son, threw his arms around him and kissed him. Rejoicing greatly, the father called his servants to come with the best robe, a ring for his finger and sandals for his feet. They killed the fattened calf, had a feast and celebrated his homecoming.

Meanwhile, the older son was working in the field. When he caught wind of what had transpired, he was livid. The sound of music and dancing made him enraged and he refused to participate in the party. He told his father how disappointed he was in the treatment of his once lost brother, now safe at home. The father reminded the elder son of his forever presence with him, the safe protection of his inheritance, and pleaded with him to celebrate and be glad that his brother was home.

In this parable Jesus is emphasizing the gift of forgiving grace. The emphasis is on the extravagant, prodigal love the Father has for both of his sons, the wayward and the righteous. The portrayal of the father running to greet the lost son is a powerful image of the initiation of God. He's got his eyes peeled on us 24/7, never turning or walking away. Whether bidden or not bidden, he is always present. He stands on the porch of heaven and traverses the landscape watching, waiting and wondering when the lost will come to his senses and turn back home.

The reality of God the initiator is a life-changer. When we come to our senses and turn back home to our heavenly Father we can ALWAYS count on his outstretched arms of grace to greet us. Always. The Triune God has an infatuation for us that never stops, never ends, never stalls, never fails. He awaits our glance homeward and then he outraces us with gifts of grace, forgiveness, and peace.

Behold Jesus locking eyes with yours; believe you are deserving of his unconditional love; belong to the fellowship of the strident wayward and the penitent homeward; and become a lover to the lost in Jesus name.

Day 21: Friday

❦

The Mustard Seed, Yeast, Treasure and Pearl

Read: Matthew 13: 31-33; 44-46

The parables of the mustard seed, the yeast, the hidden treasure and the pearl of great price are all about the kingdom of heaven. The mustard seed, even though it's the smallest of all seeds, when planted in the field it grows to be the largest of garden plants, becoming a tree for the birds of the air to perch in its branches. The yeast, when mixed into a large amount of flour, is worked into the dough for the rising of delicious bread. Both the mustard seed and the yeast are explosive in value to that which it impacts. So is the message of the gospel in comparison to any other human philosophy.

The hidden treasure found in a field brings about joy to the land owner. When the merchant discovers fine pearls of great value, he sells everything else he has in order to buy one. Small and insignificant, but larger than life in the kingdom of heaven, each of these metaphors depict the impact of the kingdom Jesus ushers in with glory and delight. The treasure and pearls describe the inestimable value of the kingdom, worth giving up everything else to acquire. The treasure is eternal life found only through salvation in Jesus Christ; the pearl is the love of Christ, when discovered there's no need to keep looking for any other substitute. In every parable, Jesus is offering his outstretched arms of grace.

These four parables are exquisitely spoken by Jesus, and packed with powerful truths. It's amazing to notice how the gospel of Jesus Christ changes everything, just like seeds and yeast transform their environments. And, the gospel of the Kingdom of heaven is a treasure beyond comparison, with the pearl of great price being nothing else but the fullness of being known and loved by God in Christ.

With the luxury of insight from hindsight, we can look back and around these stories being heard and received for the first time. Jesus enters the scene and uses the term Kingdom of heaven, but it's articulated in a brand new way. Over and over again, Jesus uses one metaphor or comparison or parable after another. His hope is that eventually his followers, especially his closest disciples, will finally "get it" and see once and for all that he is the King of this Kingdom then, now, and for all eternity.

When you hear the phrase 'kingdom of heaven' can you grasp it in your heart and mind? How well do you understand that not only are we to experience kingdom living here on earth, but we also await the fullest consummation of the kingdom with Jesus' second coming and our eternal glory? Kingdom of heaven is both already (here) and not yet (glory), so it's totally understandable why the disciples would be confused. It's a hard one to grasp!

That's why we must behold Jesus coming to establish his kingdom; believe in his eternal kingdom; belong to his kingdom circle; and become a kingdom builder.

Day 22: Saturday

❧

The Talents

Read: Matthew 25: 14-30

The Parable of the Talents is also a Kingdom parable, designed to portray those who understand God's desire for our fruitfulness in life. Those who think they know more about God than they truly do, end up missing out on the greatest of all gift of eternal life. The contrast is stark and the outcome is either blessed or bleak depending on where one lands in stewarding talents received and assigned by God.

The story is about a man who before heading out on a long journey calls his servants together, and entrusts his property to them while he's away. To one he gave five talents, to another he gave two talents, and to the third he gives one talent, each according to his ability. Then he went on his journey. The one with five talents put his money to work and gains five more. The one with two talents did likewise and gains two more. But the one with one talent dug a hole and buried his master's money.

After a long time had passed, the master of those servants came home and settled accounts with them. The man with the five talents brought those back and five more. The one with two did likewise and presented to the master two more. Both men's stewardship pleased the King, "Well done, good and faithful servant. You have been faithful with a few things, I will put you in charge of many things. Come and share your master's happiness." However, the one with one talent simply brought that one talent back, thinking the master was a hard man, harvesting where he did not sow and gathering where he did not scatter seed. The talent was taken from him and given to those who had more.

That "worthless servant" was then thrown outside into the darkness, where there was weeping and gnashing of teeth. This harsh punishment was brought upon by his bizarre rationale and illogical conclusions. His choices kept him out of the Kingdom. But, the reality of the Kingdom is that it won't be for everyone. Some will choose to say yes to God's invitation, initiation, and intention, while others will simply reject God and his ways. Therefore, everything we have has come from and belongs to God, and is to be stewarded with generosity, shared for the glory of God and offered as a blessing to others.

How well are you stewarding all you've been entrusted to for God's glory? Is there a portion of your talents you're hiding from the Father's heart? We all long to someday hear, "Well done, good and faithful servant!" as we're ushered into God's Kingdom forever. In the meantime, it's best to steward and multiply that which we've been entrusted to care for in this life.

Today, openly receive all that God's outstretched arms of grace offers. Behold the generosity of Jesus; believe that you are richly blessed to be a blessing; belong to all good and faithful stewards; and become a servant who desires nothing more than to please the Master forever.

Forth Sunday in Lent

Sunday Readings for Personal Reflection

Sabbath rest is your soul's first priority today. Cease from your work week and find rest in God alone. Worship with your faith community and remember together Jesus' sacrificial life of love. Celebrate your life in Christ and embrace your true identity in Him. As you spend time alone with God in your prayer closet, consider reviewing and prayerfully reflecting upon the following Lenten readings for this Sunday. They are taken from The Revised Common Lectionary (Vanderbilt Divinity Library) and are listed in Years A, B, and C, depending on the "cycle" for this church year. Consult resources from your local church, denomination, or the worldwide web to determine which readings/church year are most appropriate. Or, simply choose one of the groupings below and meditate on the richness of God's Word...I'm sure God will be pleased with your desires no matter what grouping you read.

Fourth Sunday in Lent - Year A

1 Samuel 16:1-13
Psalm 23
Ephesians 5:8-14
John 9:1-41

Fourth Sunday in Lent - Year B

Numbers 21:4-9
Psalm 107:1-3, 17-22
Ephesians 2:1-10
John 3:14-21

Fourth Sunday in Lent - Year C

Joshua 5:9-12
Psalm 32
2 Corinthians 5:16-21
Luke 15:1-3, 11b-32

Day 23: Monday

Words of Forgiveness

Read: John 8: 1-11

"If anyone is without sin, let him be the first to throw a stone at her." This was Jesus' incredible response to the Pharisees who brought the woman caught in adultery to him. They paraded her in front of a group of bystanders and tried to trap Jesus with their theology examination. "In the law of Moses, we are commanded to stone such women. What do you say?" One can only imagine how they stood there with their arms folded, a snarky pose of bullying on their part – to both the woman and Jesus.

Instead of replying to their intimidation, Jesus merely bent down and began writing something in the sand with his fingers. We don't know what he wrote, but he used this response to their continual inquisition.

In between two recorded instances of Jesus stooping down to the ground and writing in the dirt he invites whoever is without sin to stone the sinful woman. Slowly the crowd dissipates one person at a time. The elders left first, followed by the others, leaving only Jesus with the woman.

He asked her, "Where are your accusers? Has no one condemned you?" She replied with a simple, "No one, sir." "Then neither do I condemn you...go now and leave your life of sin," Jesus declared. And with that simple word of forgiveness she is released of her sin by the Savior of the world. With his outstretched arms of grace, Jesus generously extends forgiveness to one in need.

What is it about Jesus' repeated offer of forgiveness, without any need for remuneration beyond the acknowledgement of sin? No shame or guilt, no punishment or recourse. Simply the recognition of one's ways and ascent to the wrongdoing, and Jesus covers the rest. Each time he pardons the sinner he is upsetting the system of justice. The Pharisees were self-declared watchdogs of the Law, and they were committed to bring punitive damage to all who would step outside the Law. So, to make the woman caught in adultery stand before her peers was nothing short of public ridicule...but to them, it was necessary recompense.

Jesus associated with sinners. This was in keeping with his mission and ministry. To those who would repent of their sin, he offered the free gift of forgiveness. To repent is to feel or express regret or remorse for one's actions, to simply acknowledge the truth about oneself even and especially when one has done something counter to the will of God. It's turning around to the true heart, no more cover-up.

What is your attitude toward a known sinner? What is your attitude toward your own known sin? Without casting a single stone, receive instead the forgiveness of Jesus and be set free.

Behold the One who came to reset the Law and the Prophets with the Gospel of loving forgiveness; believe in the truth that will always set you free; belong to the community of the forgiven; become a forgiving lover too.

Day 24: Tuesday

❧

Words of Grace

Read: Luke 7: 36-50

One of the Pharisees invited Jesus to a dinner party. He accepted and ate with Simon the Pharisee, and with all the guests who were assembled. A woman who had "lived a sinful life" in that town was also present, and she brought with her an alabaster jar of perfume. She poured out that perfume onto Jesus' feet, and as she was weeping, she wet his feet with her tears, kissing and wiping them with her hair.

When Simon saw this unusual display of affection, he thought, "If this man were a prophet, he would know who is touching him and what kind of woman she is – that she is a sinner." Knowing his thoughts, Jesus answered, "Simon, I have something to tell you" and then proceeded to use a story to expose the truth. It was about two men owing money to a lender, one owing a large sum of five hundred denarii and the other owing fifty. As the lender cancels the debts of both, Jesus asks him, "Who would love him more?" Simon answered, "I suppose the one who had the bigger debt."

Simon answered the question correctly but missed the whole point. Obviously, the woman at Jesus' feet loved him more because her many sins were forgiven. Grace was freely extended to the One who extended grace to her. In contrast, there weren't even the customary expressions of grace extended to Jesus when he entered Simon's home: water to wash his feet; a kiss on the cheek to welcome his guest; or oil on his head to bless his coming. But the woman hasn't stopped kissing Jesus' feet.

The woman's many sins were forgiven graciously and generously by Jesus. The Pharisee continued to sin by hardening his heart to the love of Jesus and is the one who "has been forgiven little because he loves little." But to the woman, her sins were forgiven and her faith saved her, so she was granted peace.

To love little was never a part of Jesus' life or service to others. His love was granted overtly and with nothing shy of generosity. Jesus lavished love through the gift of grace. Grace was extended to all, but not all who heard him received his grace. He always offered and never withheld it, no matter what. Divine grace forgives sin, regenerates the heart, and sanctifies the life of those who receive this transforming and totally undeserved gift. God's outstretched arms of grace offer rich, unmerited favor, granted to sinners and saints alike, and always full of blessings to those who believe.

As a recipient of God's grace, what is your response to Jesus, the Author of Divine Grace? How will your gratitude to God for the free gift of his grace affect how you extend grace to another? Love large and not little, dear friend!

Behold Jesus generously granting grace; believe once more the transformational power of grace; belong to the company of grace recipients; and become a person of grace to all.

Day 25: Wednesday

❧

Words of Peace

Read: John 14: 15-31

"Peace I leave with you; my peace I give you. I do not give to you as the world gives. Do not let your hearts be troubled and do not be afraid." These were some of Jesus' most comforting words to the disciples as he prepares them for his inevitable departure. They were his parting words, an important segment of his farewell speech heading to the cross, and they were wrapped around the provision of the Holy Spirit after he departs their presence.

Jesus promised his disciples to give them "another Counselor" to be with them forever – the Spirit of truth. Why? Because he loved them so much and he wanted them to continue to obey him long after he left their world. He pledges, "I will not leave you as orphans; I will come to you." The Holy Spirit, sent by the Father in the name of Jesus, "will teach you all things and will remind you of everything I have said to you." This gift is another expression of his outstretched arms of grace.

Jesus offers his peace everywhere he goes, even to the very end when he promises to comfort his disciples in their grief at the time of his departure, "I have told you these things so that in me you may have peace" (John 16: 33). And, he offers peace as he enters the place where the disciples gather after his crucifixion, death and resurrection, "Peace be with you!" (John 20: 19).

The peace that Jesus promises is granted by the presence and power of the Holy Spirit. God's peace is not something that's manufactured by human effort or desire. It's not to be found in the world that surrounds us, nor is it found in that which we seek to have as an alternative to the Spirit. We don't find peace in political decisions, in times of warfare success, in business enterprise, or in athletic, academic, or any other form of accomplishment or acumen. True peace only comes from God.

The peace of Christ is to "rule our hearts" (Col. 3: 15) since we are called to be filled with the peace of God which "transcends all understanding, guarding our hearts and minds in Christ Jesus" (Phil. 4:7). During times of greeting one another in worship we offer each other "the peace of Christ" as a response to the Word, in the preparation for the offering and the Eucharist. And, in our fellowship with one another, we extend peace as an ongoing reminder that we are representatives of the Prince of Peace.

Jesus grants us peace in the midst of a tumultuous world. Will you go first to Jesus for the peace you long to embrace? Receive the Holy Spirit, the promised Counselor, who will guide you into peace.

Behold Jesus in his provision of peace for your troubled soul; believe in the gospel of peace found solely in Jesus; belong to those who genuinely pass the peace; and become a peace-maker forever.

Day 26: Thursday

❧

Words of Joy

Read: John 2: 1-11; Luke 14: 15-24

Joy in the presence of Jesus was often the outcome for those who believed his message and followed his lead. It wasn't necessarily a feel-good- happiness, but instead it was filled with meaning and significance to all who were in his presence. One can only imagine the joy of being with Jesus as he performed his first public miracle at the wedding in Cana of Galilee. He revealed his glory in such a tremendous way, through the turning of water into wine.

It's fascinating to note that it was Jesus' mother who noticed that the wine was gone. Her comment "They have no wine" stirred Jesus up and he replied, "Dear woman, why do you involve me? My time has not yet come." But Mary, with her spiritual perception, simply said to the servants present, "Do whatever he tells you." So the six stone water jars were filled with water at Jesus' command, not for the customary ceremonial washing, but instead for all of it to be changed into wine.

Fine wine, we must note. The master of the banquet said to the bridegroom, "Everyone brings out the choice wine first and then the cheaper wine after the guests have had too much to drink, but you have saved the best until now." Jesus made premium wine from the simple water in the jugs, nothing short of offering the best. We can't help but to chuckle to ourselves that of course he would make the best!

Jesus' outstretched arms of grace performed this miracle of joy. His arms of love would extend many times hence to miraculously transform lives. The offering of well water in simple jars of clay would be multiplied throughout his earthly ministry. Prompted by the Spirit in every circumstance, Jesus evoked change everywhere he traveled. Those who welcomed his gifts of love would all become new from the inside out. Thus the meaning of the parable of the great banquet: to taste joy for all eternity. "Blessed is the one who will eat at the feast in the kingdom of God."

Joy is given to us by the Spirit no matter the circumstances of our lives. Joy is birthed in the heart and soul of the believer who finds contentment in any situation. Joy is evidenced whenever God is given the glory for all gifts large and small, easy and hard, even the good and bad. For Jesus, joy was found in children, in revealed truth, in divine paradox, in repentant hearts, in community with his friends, in prayerfulness with his Father, and even as he prepared for the cross.

Will you choose joy no matter the circumstances of your life today? Will you trust the Spirit to fill you with his joy despite the status of your feelings, relationships, health or wealth?

Behold the joy of the Lord; believe in the possibility of joy; belong to the eternal banquet feast; and become joyful in Jesus, the One who miraculously turns your ordinary jars of water into fine wine.

Day 27: Friday

❧

Words of Hope

Read: John 5: 1-15

"Do you want to get well?" Jesus asked the man who had been an invalid for thirty eight years. One would think his response would be, "Of course I want to be well!" But instead, the man responds, "I have no one to help me into the pool where the water is stirred. While I am trying to get in, someone else goes down ahead of me." Was this an excuse? A rationale? A legitimate argument? Or, simply the truth, at least as he knew it.

For nearly four decades this man had been living in Jerusalem near the Sheep Gate, by a pool called Bethesda, which was surrounded by five covered colonnades. Over the years many others had come to the pool for healing: the blind, the lame, and the paralyzed. This man had obviously seen the miraculous healings of others, but for whatever reason he wasn't one of the healed.

Until Jesus arrives on the scene. Jesus very simply urged him to "Get up! Pick up your mat and walk" into the pool. At once the man was cured. When confronted by the Jews who were present that day, which happened to also be the Sabbath, he could not distinguish Jesus from the crowd since he slipped away so swiftly. All he knew was that Someone had finally said to him the words of hope that powerfully transformed his life, "Pick up your mat and walk."

These words of hope, planted immediately in the heart of the invalid, produced miraculous results. Even later in the day when Jesus found the healed man in the temple, he continues to press hope into his heart by exhorting him, "You are well again. Stop sinning or something worse may happen to you." Later, in Luke 18, we see a blind man begging on the side of the road and he calls out to Jesus for healing and upon receiving it is filled with contagious hope.

Hope is indeed infectious. It's the starting line for the race ahead, the fuel for every mile of the marathon, and the delightful refreshment of the finish line. It's what keeps us moving forward in our faith, and it's what sustains us in our love. Hope is the catalyst for life-giving words, the impetus for good works, and the end result of the life well lived. Without hope we have no passion for developing our character into the image of Christ. Without hope we have no reason for living, and we become satisfied at the side of the pool of healing, but never stepping in for ourselves.

What do you want from Jesus' outstretched arms of grace today? What part of your life needs to be revolutionized by hope?

Behold Jesus saying "Get up and walk" forward; believe that you too can be healed of your long-term heartache; belong to the church of the hopeful; and become one who freely spreads words of hope to all who cross your path each new day.

Day 28: Saturday

❦

Words of Love

Read: Mark 10: 17-31; Luke 10: 38-42

"*One thing* I ask of the Lord, this is what I seek: that I may dwell in the house of the Lord all the days of my life, to gaze upon the beauty of the Lord..." (Psalm 27: 4) The Apostle Paul writes of the *one thing* to do: pressing on to the upward call of God in Christ Jesus (Phil. 3:14). Peter also writes, the *one thing* to remember is that with the Lord one day is a thousand years (2 Peter 3: 8, 9), demonstrating God's longsuffering in the process of salvation, extending patiently his outstretched arms of grace.

Here in the gospels, Jesus says to the rich young man, "*One thing* you lack..." and to Martha, Jesus answers, "Only *one thing* is needed." *One thing*. Just one.

What is the *one thing*? Loving devotion to the Lord. Jesus challenges the rich young man, "One thing you lack. Go sell everything you have and give to the poor, and you will have treasure in heaven. Then come, follow me." His great wealth stood in the way of his desire for God. He stays with his wealth, which leads Jesus to the commentary, "How hard it is for the rich to enter the kingdom of God! It is easier for a camel to go through the eye of a needle than for a rich man to enter the kingdom of God."

For Martha, she was distracted from attentiveness to Jesus by all the preparations of the household. She speaks up about the work and how her sister Mary has left her to herself. "Tell her to help me!" she demands. Jesus comforts Martha with a reminder of the one thing that matters most, and "Mary has chosen what is better." Jesus much preferred the loving consideration of Mary instead of the distracted inattentiveness of Martha.

The "one thing" that matters most to Jesus is love. It's love that brings one to repentance, forgiveness and salvation. It's love that opens the door to a life of listening attentively to the invitations of the Lord for faithful obedience and sacrificial service. It's love that delights in the empowerment of the Spirit for all of life, and which envelops hope and faith, mercy and grace, truth and joy.

What are the many things that hinder you from attentiveness to the *one thing* that matters most? Is it the many things of your profession and the acquisition of possessions; it is your relationships and the desire you have to please or power over others; or is it something else or something more? Identify that which stands in the way of you enjoying the *one thing* Jesus invites: a deep, unending love for God.

Behold the audience of One; believe the One Gospel of grace; belong to the One True God and all who call him Lord; and become more like the One Jesus, who calls you by name and desires to love and be loved by the one and only you.

Fifth Sunday in Lent

Sunday Readings for Personal Reflection

Sabbath rest is your soul's first priority today. Cease from your work week and find rest in God alone. Worship with your faith community and remember together Jesus' sacrificial life of love. Celebrate your life in Christ and embrace your true identity in Him. As you spend time alone with God in your prayer closet, consider reviewing and prayerfully reflecting upon the following Lenten readings for this Sunday. They are taken from The Revised Common Lectionary (Vanderbilt Divinity Library) and are listed in Years A, B, and C, depending on the "cycle" for this church year. Consult resources from your local church, denomination, or the worldwide web to determine which readings/church year are most appropriate. Or, simply choose one of the groupings below and meditate on the richness of God's Word...I'm sure God will be pleased with your desires no matter what grouping you read.

Fifth Sunday in Lent - Year A

Ezekiel 37:1-14
Psalm 130
Romans 8:6-11
John 11:1-45

Fifth Sunday in Lent - Year B

Jeremiah 31:31-34
Psalm 51:1-12 *or Psalm 119:9-16*
Hebrews 5:5-10
John 12:20-33

Fifth Sunday in Lent - Year C

Isaiah 43:16-21
Psalm 126
Philippians 3:4b-14
John 12:1-8

Day 29: Monday

❧

Among Children

Read: Mark 9: 33-37; 10: 13-16

Jesus loves the little children, all the children of the world. Red, yellow, black and white, they are precious in his sight. Jesus loves the little children of the world. If you've begun to sing along, that's a good sign. When Jesus was confronting the pride of his disciples, who were arguing with one another about who is the greatest, he chose a child to make his point. It wasn't enough for him to merely say, "If anyone wants to be first, he must be the very last, the servant of all."

He put an exclamation point on his teaching when he took a little child and had him stand in their midst. Then, he welcomed the child with outstretched arms of grace and said to them, "Whoever welcomes one of these little children in my name welcomes me." How they treated a child was an indicator to Jesus as to whether or not there was pride in their heart. Those who stooped down to the child's level and extended their arms were lovers, in contrast to any who would stand prideful, aloof or dismissive.

When people were bringing their little children to Jesus for him to touch them, the disciples rebuked them. When Jesus saw this he was indignant and said to them, "Let the little children come to me, and do not hinder them, for the kingdom of God belongs to such as these…anyone who will not receive the kingdom of God like a little child will not enter it." Then he took the children in his arms, put his hands on them, and blessed them. A powerful expression of his love.

It's delightful to consider the many ways Jesus comes alongside children. He used a child's loaves and fish to feed five thousand hungry souls. He healed children, cast demons out of them, and even raised a little girl from the dead. Children joined the chorus "Hosanna to the Son of David!" as their expression of love and gratitude for Jesus. He had a magnetic heart toward children and he encouraged his disciples to live likewise, welcoming little children, receiving and blessing them in his and their presence.

What is your attitude toward the children in your sphere of influence? Are they a nuisance, disturbance, or hindrance to your life? Or, are they welcomed with outstretched arms of grace into your midst, embraced as an especially beloved child of God? Are they treated as a gift, like sugar for your soul? Are you able to join Jesus in inviting them into your life to challenge your pride and open up your heart to the kingdom of heaven here and now? Consider prayerfully how God might be tapping you on the shoulder of your heart in regard to your relationship with your own children.

Behold Jesus among the little children and rejoice; believe once more how welcoming children is kingdom living; belong to those who love all God's children; become childlike in your heart today.

Day 30: Tuesday

❧

Among Seekers

Read: Luke 19: 1-10

Earnest seekers did many unusual things to get close to Jesus. Some pushed their way through crowds to touch the hem of his garment. Others opened the canopy of the roof of a home to drop a paralytic friend into the center of the room so Jesus could heal him. In the story today we see Zacchaeus the tax collector climbing up a sycamore-fig tree to see Jesus as he was coming his way. Very creative for the short man who knew he could not see Jesus because of the crowd.

When Jesus reached the spot where Zacchaeus was up in the tree, he noticed him and said, "Zacchaeus, come down immediately. I must stay at your house today." So he came down and welcomed Jesus with gladness of heart into his home. It must have been the thrill of his lifetime! But, when all of the towns' people saw this they began to mutter silly slander, "He has gone to be the guest of a sinner."

Not a gross sinner for very long, however. Zacchaeus was so delighted to be in Jesus' presence that he was convicted of his sin and openly confessed how he wanted to make things right. He said to Jesus, "Look, Lord! Here and now I give half of my possessions to the poor, and if I have cheated anybody out of anything, I will pay back four times the amount." The tax collector was set free to become a child of God, releasing his well-earned possessions to the poor, and paying back any ill-earned money four times the original amount. What a great picture of repentance – a total turn around for this "sinner."

No wonder Jesus loved hanging out with sinners! It was the sinners who knew they were in need of a Savior. The sinners were the ones who were broken, sick, hungry, poor of spirit, troubled of mind, greedy of gain, and prideful of heart. Those who were focused on the Law more than grace, pointed fingers of judgment and closed their hearts to the gospel. To be accused of associating with sinners was a badge of honor for Jesus, for he came to seek and to save what was lost.

Zacchaeus was found and saved by Jesus on that great day of joy. Jesus declares, "Today salvation has come to this house." Zacchaeus believed and was considered righteous in God's eyes, and was generous with his money, magnanimously offering it to the poor. The Son of Man declares this of Zacchaeus: he once was lost, but now is found.

Can you recall the time when you were seeking Jesus? When you received his outstretched arms of grace? Perhaps you remember the joy and zeal you had as a new believer? Reclaim that once more!

Behold the beauty of the Lord Jesus with a seekers heart; believe the transformation he desired for you then and now; belong to the fellowship of those who continue to seek Jesus with all their heart, soul, mind and strength; become a curious seeker once again, even if it means climbing a tree to see better.

Day 31: Wednesday

❧

Among Betrayers

Read: Matthew 26: 14-17; Luke 22: 1-6

Judas Iscariot. His first name has become synonymous with one word: betrayal.

"What are you willing to give me if I hand him over to you?" he asks the chief priests. "Thirty silver coins" was all they had; and all Judas apparently needed. So they watched him until he was able to hand Jesus over to them. Jesus knew it was coming, for when they were reclining at table, he foretold it by saying "Woe to that man who betrays the Son of Man!" Judas had a rather ambiguous reply, "Surely not I, Rabbi?" Jesus answered him, "Yes, it is you."

Luke tells us that "Satan entered Judas" and that's what led to his going to the chief priests and officers of the temple guard to discuss with them how he might betray Jesus. Of course they were delighted at the possibility that one of the Twelve would make such an offer. This made their job much easier. And, Judas became a bit richer. But only for a short time...those coins must have burned a hole in his pocket.

Since we know the rest of the story, we know that this denial killed Judas too...he was a wreck. For when he saw that Jesus was actually being condemned to death, he was seized with remorse and returned the thirty silver coins to the chief priests and the elders. "I have sinned," he said, "for I have betrayed innocent blood." So he threw the money into the temple and left to hang himself. How incredibly sad to be a betrayer, even one with penitent sorrow after all was said and done.

If you've ever been betrayed by someone you thought was for you, you know how much this hurts. One can only imagine how Jesus must have felt, despite this plot being a part of the God-intended meta-narrative. Judas was one of his twelve disciples, who had traveled with him and watched him perform miracles of healing and grace. He had interacted with the other disciples daily and for a few very significant years. Most likely with obedience as his regular track record, this time he fell into the hands of evil and was used as a tool of Satan in this life-destroying betrayal.

Betrayals are rare but costly to any relationship. Like Judas, they most often come at the instigation of the enemy who wants to destroy every healthy relationship. And, in vulnerable moments, even the best intentioned person can be curtailed and led astray. When the enemy whispers in the ears of the most susceptible, his trickery can quickly create interpersonal upheaval and destruction.

But, we know Jesus didn't treat Judas any differently as a result of his betrayal. We still see him with outstretched arms of grace toward Judas, just as he always had offered.

Behold Jesus exhibiting unconditional love toward his Judas; believe in the redemptive value of repentance; belong to those who are accused and betrayed because of Jesus; become strengthened in the power of Christ.

Day 32: Thursday

❧

Among Deniers

Read: Luke 22: 54-62

"Before the rooster crows today, you will disown me three times – yes, deny three times that you know me, Peter." These were shocking words from Jesus to his much beloved Simon. His retort to Jesus, "Lord, I am ready to go with you to prison and to death" was genuinely spoken, but never came true.

Instead, by the charcoal fire pit, after they seized Jesus and led him away and into the house of the high priest, Peter sat with the others. In the middle of the courtyard he was confronted by a young servant girl seated near the firelight. She looked carefully at him and said, "This man was with him." But he denied it. As quickly as that, he spoke his first renunciation.

A little later someone else saw him and said, "You also are one of them." But he denied it a second time. About an hour later, another asserted, "Certainly this fellow was with him, for he is a Galilean." But Peter replied, "Man, I don't know what you're talking about!" Just after this exasperated response the rooster crowed. The Lord turned and looked straight at Peter. Then Peter remembered what Jesus had said to him at the supper table. And he went outside and wept bitterly.

Peter's impetuous denials were typical to his rather spontaneous way of living. Peter was always the most passionate one of the Twelve. He was the one who tried walking on water but fell instead. He was the one who seemed quickest to speak and slowest to listen. He was the one who wanted to erect shelters at the transfiguration. He was the focus of the foot washing ceremony when he first denies needing his feet washed and then asks that not only his feet but his hands and head be washed as well.

Peter was a leader among the disciples, his name always listed first. He was in the core group of three disciples, including James and John. He was the first to perceive Jesus as Messiah, first to be called by name by Jesus, first to confess his sinfulness, and first to promise never to desert Jesus. Jesus made a radical difference in Peter's life, and his allegiance and alliance seemed unbreakable. Until his denial.

Jesus loves Peter and keeps extending his outstretched arms of grace to his beloved friend. He reinstates Peter post-resurrection at another charcoal fire pit, this time by the water's edge when Peter three times says that he loves Jesus and promises to feed his sheep and tend his lambs. From the fire pit of disgraceful denial to the fireplace of disarming devotion: Peter, dear Peter, reinstated companion of Jesus despite taking a few impulsive tumbles along the way.

Behold Jesus loving his hotheaded denier back into intimate friendship; believe that even a denial of Jesus can be forgiven; belong to the fallen who stand once more because of the forgiving cross of Christ; become an affectionate lover of God, Father, Son and Holy Spirit, even after the rooster crows thrice.

Day 33: Friday

⌘

Among Enemies

Read: Luke 23: 1-25 and John 19: 1-16

Even among his most defiant enemies, Jesus extends his outstretched arms of grace.

Imagine standing among the throngs who were demanding that a criminal previously thrown in prison for insurrection and murder be set free and instead replaced by Jesus, the One who previously restored life and miraculously freed those who were shackled by disease, poverty, injustice, and demon possession. The crowds were filled with enemies of Jesus who stirred up the chant to "Crucify him!" and all forms of godly reason and fair rationale were gone with the shouts of hatred scattered by the wind.

Release Barabbas and crucify Jesus? This made no sense whatsoever, first to Herod, then to Pilate, but among the enemy crowd it was the best alternative replacement they could demand. So the leaders surrendered Jesus to the will of the crowd. "Father, forgive them, for they do not know what they are doing" is the best response of all, spoken freely, generously, and open-heartedly by Jesus.

Enemies are such because of perceptions or misperceptions held firmly and one-sidedly. Active opposition or blatant hostility doesn't just come out of nowhere…it originates from deeply held convictions about why a person or philosophy would be hated or despised. To have an enemy is to create a tall barrier which is impenetrable and impossible to navigate unilaterally. Only in relationship can an enemy be won (back) to allegiance and alliance without creating further damage.

Those who kept shouting "Crucify him!" had no justification for their demand, except prejudice. They didn't like what they saw in Jesus of Nazareth, and the accumulation of their pent up frustration reached a boiling point unsustainable by the leaders. The ground swell of opposition had gained such strong momentum that the entrance into that first Holy Week was cascading upon the disciples and all other devoted but now depleted followers of Jesus. They were grossly outnumbered by the haters in the pack of wolves now descending on the humble Lamb of God, to flog, beat, and crown him with thorns.

There is little anyone can do to fight defiant hostility

and unreasonable predisposition. So, as the leaders surrendered to the crowds, Jesus simultaneously surrenders to the Father. Instead of putting up a fight, he willingly accepts the way of suffering, beginning with the physical carrying of his designated, splinter-filled, heavy-burdened cross up the hill to the place called The Skull. There would be his final breath of life, brought on because of the words of the enemies who called for his crucifixion.

Behold the King of Kings and Lord of Lords; believe in the Gospel which was hated by the enemies of God; belong to those who were in the crowd and stood up for Jesus; become defiant for Truth and Love without hatred, prejudice, hostility or damnation ever on your lips or in your heart toward any other.

Day 34: Saturday

❧

Among Doubters

Read: John 20: 24-31

Tomorrow is the beginning of Holy Week. Even with all that will transpire there will be those among us who remain doubtful that all of this ever transpired in the first place. The historical record of Jesus, including the biblical accounts by eyewitnesses whose writing would be protected for thousands of years, won't be enough for the doubters and the skeptics among us. In every generation, and sometimes even among our existing generation, there will always be doubters who raise objections to the Gospel.

This is nothing new. Thomas, one of Jesus' original disciples, missed the first time Jesus appeared to the disciples as they gathered together behind locked doors, when he showed them his hands and side. The disciples were overjoyed when they saw the Lord, and Jesus blessed them, "Peace be with you! As the Father has sent me, I am sending you." Then he breathed on them and said, "Receive the Holy Spirit. If you forgive anyone his sins, they are forgiven; if you do not forgive them, they are not forgiven."

So when the disciples tell Thomas about this encounter, he responds, "Unless I see the nail marks in his hands and put my finger where the nails were, and put my hand into his side, I will not believe it." A week later Jesus returns to be with them and standing among them says, "Peace be with you!" and immediately turns to Thomas. He invites him to put his finger into his nail scarred hand and his hand into his pierced side. Thomas replies, "My Lord and my God!" and believes.

Unflappable Jesus isn't thrown off by Thomas' doubts. In fact, with outstretched arms of grace he invites Thomas' doubts to be released by faith in the truth of his nail-scarred sacrifice in his behalf. Thomas' doubts were welcomed by Jesus and addressed openly without any threat to his ultimate belief. By embracing Thomas and his doubts, Jesus speaks directly and forthrightly the Truth that sets him free.

What do you do with doubters who surround you or doubts that simmer within you? They are there with a purpose: to be proven real or wrong. Otherwise, they remain unattended and eat away the lining of the soul and like a cancer will keep fracturing our heart from our mind. By addressing doubts and exposing them, one can accompany each doubt with facts or affect, space or time, with mystery or faith. When a person's uncertainty is embraced and dealt with one question at a time, each doubt is respected for what it truly has become. Doubt is not the opposite or the enemy of our faith. It takes holy and courageous boldness to face our doubts, whether or not they will ever be replaced with faith.

Behold Jesus initiating toward Thomas and his doubts; believe in the gospel amidst your ponderings; belong to those who ask hard and clarifying questions; become a believer who isn't afraid to doubt nor is shattered to consider others who doubt.

And now we proceed to the greatest story ever revealed...Holy Week: the road paved with faith to Calvary, the empty tomb, and beyond.

Palm Sunday

Sunday Readings for Personal Reflection

Sabbath rest is your soul's first priority today on this Palm Sunday. Cease from your work week and find rest in God alone. Worship with your faith community and remember together Jesus' sacrificial life of love, especially as you contemplate the forthcoming events of Holy Week. Celebrate your life in Christ and embrace your true identity in Him. As you spend time alone with God in your prayer closet, consider reviewing and prayerfully reflecting upon the following Lenten readings for this Sunday. They are taken from The Revised Common Lectionary (Vanderbilt Divinity Library) and are listed in Years A, B, and C, depending on the "cycle" for this church year. Consult resources from your local church, denomination, or the worldwide web to determine which readings/church year are most appropriate. Or, simply choose one of the groupings below and meditate on the richness of God's Word...I'm sure God will be pleased with your desires no matter what grouping you read.

Palm Sunday - Year A

Psalm 118:1-2, 19-29

Matthew 21:1-11

Isaiah 50: 4-9a; Psalm 31: 9-16; Phil. 2: 5-11; Matt. 26: 14-27: 66 or 27: 11-54

Palm Sunday - Year B

Psalm 118:1-2, 19-29

Mark 11:1-11 *or John 12:12-16*

Isaiah 50: 4-9a; Psalm 31: 9-16; Phil. 2:5-11; Mark 14: 1-15:47 or 15: 1-39 (40-47)

Palm Sunday - Year C

Psalm 118:1-2, 19-29

Luke 19:28-40

Isaiah 50: 4-9a; Psalm 31: 9-16; Phil. 2: 5-11; Luke 22: 14-23: 56 or 23: 1-49

Day 35: Monday

Monday after Palm Sunday

Read: Matthew 21: 1-11; Mark 11: 1-11; Luke 19: 28-44

A borrowed donkey as the chosen form of transportation for Jesus to enter Jerusalem? Yes, as it was prophetically foretold and now fulfilled in their midst. "See, your king comes to you, gentle and riding on a donkey, on a colt, the foal of a donkey." With Jesus' specific instructions about how to secure and use the animal, he sat on the cloaks of his disciples on the back of a donkey for his triumphal entry.

Can you imagine the scene? As Jesus entered the city from the Mount of Olives, people began to gather and spread their cloaks on the road, in addition to those who spread palm branches. "Blessed is the king who comes in the name of the Lord! Peace in heaven and glory to the highest!" Nothing could keep them from their exaltation, including the Pharisees in the crowd who urged Jesus to rebuke and quiet his disciples. But he replied, "If they keep quiet, the stones will cry out."

"Blessed is the coming kingdom of our father David" they exclaimed. The crowds continued, "This is Jesus, the prophet from Nazareth in Galilee" and their shouts of joy filled the city streets with delight. Everywhere Jesus went on the humble foal he was greeted with wonderful acclaim. The crowd was thrilled with his arrival and they didn't let the stones do the crying out; they were determined to be the ones who gave voice to the "Hosanna!" greeting he certainly deserved.

But that was yesterday, when on Palm Sunday Jesus entered the city with power from on high, now expressed in his deep humility. Today we begin to settle into the drama of all dramas, the grand finale of Lent. Holy Week has descended on the city of Jerusalem and the apex of the crowd's acclamation will soon follow with their derision. Mockery, scorn, and bitter contempt will be their mood in just a few days. They swiftly shift from adoration and worship to worthless ridicule almost overnight. Why? How? For what reason? The fickle crowds who once followed his every movement, reached out to him for every possible healing, were now getting ready to dismantle his power and turn against his authority.

But Jesus continues to give of himself with outstretched arms of grace. He complies with the prophet's word and issues the request for a donkey to carry him one last time into Jerusalem as a free man. And all with full knowledge of what's in store for him later in the week. You can almost see him enduring the ride on the back of a simple donkey for the soul of the crowd. It was the best mode of transport for the King of Kings and Lord of Lords, who always led by humility, grace, wisdom and love.

Behold him being worshiped and adored; believe in the Lord's exaltation; belong to the members of the crowd who would stay faithful to the end; and become a worshiper with fresh insight and holy boldness.

———

For additional reflection today, prayerfully consider the words of this ancient Holy Week hymn, "All Glory Laud and Honor" (Orleans, 1820: Neale, 1851):

Refrain:
All glory, laud and honor,
To Thee, Redeemer, King,
To Whom the lips of children
Made sweet hosannas ring.

Thou art the King of Israel,
Thou David's royal Son,
Who in the Lord's Name comest,
The King and Blessed One.

Refrain

The company of angels
Are praising Thee on High,
And mortal men and all things
Created make reply.

Refrain

The people of the Hebrews
With palms before Thee went;
Our prayer and praise and anthems
Before Thee we present.

Refrain

To Thee, before Thy passion,
They sang their hymns of praise;
To Thee, now high exalted,
Our melody we raise.

Refrain

Thou didst accept their praises;
Accept the prayers we bring,
Who in all good delightest,
Thou good and gracious King.

Refrain

Day 36: Tuesday

Just Another Ordinary Day?

Read: Matthew 21-25

Tuesday of Holy Week is one of the fullest days for the teaching ministry of Jesus. It's one of the quieter days for religious ceremony in our day, but for Jesus it was chock full of significant work. Therefore, if you have the time to reflect on all five chapters of the Gospel of Matthew, you'll see this for yourself.

Starting in the early morning, we see him traveling and hungry, and noticing a fig tree by the side of the road, but there were no figs just leaves. So he pronounces it barren and immediately it withers. Then, he stumps those who question his authority to do such things with a quiz they fail to answer...so neither does he tell them by what authority he is doing these things. Brilliant, Jesus! I marvel at his approach.

Then, we read on to discover some of the most poignant parables: the two sons, the tenants, and the wedding banquet. All of them are about the Kingdom he is ushering in with his presence, but to those who "did not believe" (Matt. 21: 32) or "who killed the heir and took his inheritance" (Matt. 21: 38-40) or "did not deserve to come to the banquet" (Matt. 22: 8) did not make it. Each is a withered fig tree!

He continues on with exposing hypocrisy about paying taxes ("give to Caesar what is Caesar's, and to God what is God's") and misinformation about the Scriptures and the resurrection ("you do not know the Scriptures and the power of God"), followed by a question of an expert of the law, "Which is the greatest commandment?" Jesus replies with precision, "Love the Lord your God with all your heart, soul and mind…" with the second like it, "Love your neighbor as yourself." Perfect answer, Jesus.

And if that wasn't enough, on Tuesday he also proclaims to the crowds the seven woes to those who do not practice what they preach. Each of them directed specifically to the Scribes and Pharisees. These are followed by teachings about the signs of the end of all things, the day and hour remaining unknown, and underscored by three parables about "keeping watch" – the ten virgins, talents and sheep/goats.

Yes, nothing very ordinary or sublime about the Tuesday of Holy Week! It's full to overflowing, expressive of the urgency of Jesus' presence in their midst and his final words to them about why he came and the importance of the Kingdom of heaven. Reflecting on these firm teachings is yet another reminder of the outstretched arms of grace coming from Jesus: don't miss out on eternity and the explicit nature of the Kingdom of heaven. Keep watch; seize the day; say yes; remain faithful; be blessed; love!

Behold Jesus living abundantly, maximizing every possible moment; believe his warnings and embrace his teachings; belong to those who love rather than judge; and become wise, vigilant, faithful, and true.

—◦ʃʃʃ◦—

For additional reflection today, prayerfully consider the words of this ancient Holy Week hymn, "Jesus Lover of My Soul" by Charles Wesley, 1740:

Jesus, lover of my soul, let me to Thy bosom fly,
While the nearer waters roll, while the tempest still is high.
Hide me, O my Savior, hide, till the storm of life is past;
Safe into the haven guide; O receive my soul at last.

Other refuge have I none, hangs my helpless soul on Thee;
Leave, ah! leave me not alone, still support and comfort me.
All my trust on Thee is stayed, all my help from Thee I bring;
Cover my defenseless head with the shadow of Thy wing.

Wilt Thou not regard my call? Wilt Thou not accept my prayer? Lo! I sink, I faint, I fall—Lo! on Thee I cast my care; Reach me out Thy gracious hand! While I of Thy strength receive, Hoping against hope I stand, dying, and behold, I live.

Thou, O Christ, art all I want, more than all in Thee I find; Raise the fallen, cheer the faint, heal the sick, and lead the blind. Just and holy is Thy Name, I am all unrighteousness; False and full of sin I am; Thou art full of truth and grace.

Plenteous grace with Thee is found, grace to cover all my sin; Let the healing streams abound; make and keep me pure within. Thou of life the fountain art, freely let me take of Thee; Spring Thou up within my heart; rise to all eternity.

Day 37: Wednesday

❧

Silent Wednesday

Read: Mark 14: 1-11

Silent Wednesday. Known more for darkness than light. Many will gather tonight for Tenebrae service, when darkness will descend upon them through the hymns, readings and reflections calling for their heart's focus on this mid-week turning point to the drama of Holy Week. The lights are extinguishing, as the earthly life and ministry of Jesus is coming to dramatic conclusion. From Wednesday we descend even further into the dark days of denial, humiliation, and ultimate death on the cross. No turning back.

What we do know is that on this day Judas is preparing to betray Jesus. He agrees to thirty silver coins from the chief priests in return for directing them to Jesus. From then on Judas is on the watch for an opportunity to hand him over. Darkness is personified in a man with a dastardly deed to complete.

The account of Judas' preparation for betrayal is preceded by the story of Jesus in Bethany, reclining at the table of Simon the Leper. A woman came with an alabaster jar of very expensive perfume. She broke open the jar and poured the perfume on his head. Some of those present were indignant with the waste, and she was rebuked harshly. Judas was one who objected; not because he cared for the poor who could have benefited from selling the perfume, but selfishly for him as a greedy thief.

Jesus honors the woman for pouring perfume so extravagantly, calling it "a beautiful thing…to prepare for my burial." Jesus knew her heart and was pleased with her offering of love. He also knew the heart of Judas and the eventuality of his betrayal. To both Jesus extends his outstretched arms of grace, as a recipient of loving worship and as inheritor of Judas' projected duplicity and disloyalty. His freedom and faithfulness to offer love no matter what will transpire is a wonderful portrayal of the true Jesus.

We are left to presume how the remaining hours of this day are used by Jesus and his followers. One might project him walking peacefully, reflecting prayerfully, watching and waiting, noticing, listening and preparing himself for the turning points yet to come. While the plot to arrest, convict and crucify is unfolding all around him, we can only imagine how he's getting prepared for what's to come.

That's why the picture of contrast between expensive perfumes being poured out on his head is so diametrically juxtaposed with his friend selling out to the authorities in order to hand him over to death. Both are essential to his pending death. Both are crucial to the story line of this dramatic week. Both are hinges to what's to come. Both acts are indispensable to his final sacrificial drama on the cross.

Behold him resting peacefully amidst a brewing caldron of exploitation; believe in the power of the cross to stampede over death into eternal life; belong to the ones who know the full story and will mourn only so long; and become transformed from the inside out by the life-changing unconditional love of Jesus.

———

For additional reflection today, prayerfully consider the words of this ancient Holy Week hymn, "My Song Is Love Unknown" written in 1664 by Samuel Crossman:

My song is love unknown, My Savior's love to me;
Love to the loveless shown, That they might lovely be.
O who am I, That for my sake
My Lord should take Frail flesh and die?

He came from His blest throne Salvation to bestow;
But men made strange, and none The longed-for Christ
would know:

But O! my Friend, My Friend indeed,
Who at my need His life did spend.

Sometimes they strew His way, And His sweet praises sing;
Resounding all the day Hosannas to their King:
Then "Crucify!" is all their breath,
And for His death they thirst and cry.

Why, what hath my Lord done? What makes this rage and spite?
He made the lame to run, He gave the blind their sight,
Sweet injuries! Yet they at these
Themselves displease, and 'gainst Him rise.

They rise and needs will have My dear Lord made away;
A murderer they save, The Prince of life they slay,
Yet cheerful He to suffering goes,
That He His foes from thence might free.

In life no house, no home, My Lord on earth might have;
In death no friendly tomb, But what a stranger gave.
What may I say? Heav'n was his home;
But mine the tomb Wherein he lay.

Here might I stay and sing, No story so divine;
Never was love, dear King! Never was grief like Thine.
This is my Friend, in Whose sweet praise
I all my days could gladly spend.

Day 38: Thursday

❦

Maundy Thursday

Read: John 13: 1-17

Jesus knew that the time had come for him to leave this world and go to the Father. So, having loved his own who were in the world with him, he now showed them the full extent of his love.

As the evening meal was being served, he got up from the table and took off his outer clothing, and wrapped a towel around his waist. After preparing himself to serve his brothers, he poured water into a basin and began to wash his disciples' feet, drying them with a towel that was wrapped around him.

Peter didn't quite understand what was happening and initially denied Jesus the privilege. But after Jesus explained that "unless I wash you, you will have no part with me," Peter not only presented his feet, but asked that his hands and head be washed as well. To Jesus, simply holding and washing their feet was enough of a bath for his faithful followers…including the one who would deny him and even the one who would betray him. Here again we see the Lord extending his outstretched arms of grace.

When he was finished washing their feet, he explained why he had done this simple act. As their Teacher and Lord, having washed their feet, he now requested they wash one another's feet. "No servant is greater than his master, nor is a messenger greater than the one who sent him. Now that you know these things, you will be blessed if you do them." And then he proceeds to predict his upcoming betrayal and denial by two of them who had just experienced the full extent of his humble love.

By far one of the most intimate moments, the washing of the feet was one of Jesus' final expressions of love to his disciples. To hold their dirty feet in his gentle hands, pour water over them to soothe and bathe as with a cup of salvation, was all he needed to do. He simply wanted his disciples to know that his love was genuine, and his desire for them to do likewise was pure. The ministry of soul hospitality at the table, surrounding this meal, was rich and abundant for all, even for his confused betrayer. Jesus knew his time had come. His days were numbered. His legacy would live on in love.

If you've ever had your feet held and washed by

another you know how meaningful it is. Imagine Jesus stooping down in front of you, holding your worn and weary feet, looking up at your face with loving affirmation, looking down at your faithful feet, and praying blessing over your walk of faith. He knows your need for cleansing and forgiveness. He is fully aware of every heartache you hold, every pain you've suffered, every joy you've experienced, every longing your desire. Will you let him love you?

Behold the Savior kneeling lovingly and prayerfully before you; believe in the gifts of grace and mercy he delights to bestow; belong to the fellowship of foot-washed disciples; and become a disciple who is more than willing to wash another's feet in Jesus' name.

—*∿*—

For additional reflection today, prayerfully consider the words of this ancient Holy Week hymn, "What Wondrous Love Is This O My Soul" (Anonymous, 1811):

What wondrous love is this, O my soul, O my soul!
What wondrous love is this, O my soul!
What wondrous love is this that caused the Lord of bliss
To bear the dreadful curse for my soul, for my soul,
To bear the dreadful curse for my soul.

When I was sinking down, sinking down, sinking down,
When I was sinking down, sinking down,

Outstretched Arms of Grace

When I was sinking down beneath God's righteous frown,
Christ laid aside His crown for my soul, for my soul,
Christ laid aside His crown for my soul.

To God and to the Lamb, I will sing, I will sing;
To God and to the Lamb, I will sing.
To God and to the Lamb Who is the great "I Am";
While millions join the theme, I will sing, I will sing;
While millions join the theme, I will sing.

And when from death I'm free, I'll sing on, I'll sing on;
And when from death I'm free, I'll sing on.
And when from death I'm free, I'll sing and joyful be;
And through eternity, I'll sing on, I'll sing on;
And through eternity, I'll sing on.

Day 39: Friday

⸙

Good Friday

Read: John 19: 16-37

Jesus on the cross – the ultimate expression of his outstretched arms of grace!

His arms could not have been stretched out any further than when they were extended for all humanity on the cross. Simply held back on the beam that far and for so long would have been enough to endure, but with the nails piercing his hands the suffering was all the more agonizing for Jesus. The crown of thorns on his head and the nails holding his feet in place added to his injurious position. This humiliation and suffering went far beyond the washing of the disciples' feet in expressing the fullest extent of love.

Carrying his own cross, he walked with the soldiers out to The Place of the Skull, known as Golgotha. He was crucified with two others – one on each side, with Jesus in the middle. Pilate's notice was fastened above his head on the cross, "Jesus of Nazareth, The King of the Jews." The soldiers divided his clothes among them, one share for each of the four attending him. But his seamless undergarment they did not tear, and instead cast lots for it.

Near the cross stood his mother and the other women. Looking down Jesus saw his mother and the beloved disciple. He said to his mother, "Dear woman, here is your son" and from that time on this faithful disciple took her into his home and cared for her. Words came from his tired breathing, "Father forgive them" - "You will be with me in paradise" - "My God, my God, why have you forsaken me?" - "I am thirsty" - "It is finished" - "Into your hands I commit my spirit" and after a soaked sponge of wine vinegar was placed on his lips, he bowed his head and breathed his last, giving up his spirit into death.

Instead of breaking his legs to complete his demise, the soldiers pierced Jesus' side with a spear, bringing a sudden flow of blood and water. Not one of his bones was broken, as the prophet foretold, for those who search for the Living God "will look on the one they have pierced instead." And that's how it occurred. The death of Jesus was completed on the cross in the most wretched form possible.

It's hard to fathom what it would have been like to witness such cruelty. In such a short time frame Jesus went from the highly acclaimed King to the lowly despised criminal. From "Hosanna!" to "Crucify him!" in a matter of days. Even though Pilate sought to set Jesus free, the Jews kept shouting about his demise. In handing Jesus over to the will of the people, he washed his hands of his death. The drama this act sparked would be exactly as God intended...amazing love, how can it be, that Thou my God would die for me? How many present could sing that hymn of praise? Would you?

Behold the Lamb of God who takes away the sin of the world; believe the Gospel of grace poured out in the shed blood of Christ on the cross; belong to those who know Him as Savior, Lord and King; and become a fervent and faithful follower of Jesus the One who left heaven to come to earth to die so that you can have life eternal.

—◈—

For additional reflection today, prayerfully consider the words of this ancient Holy Week hymn, "O Sacred Head Now Wounded" by Bernard of Clairvaux, 1153 (an alternative hymn to consider today is "Ah, Holy Jesus, How Hast Thou Offended?"):

O sacred Head, now wounded, with grief and shame weighed down,
Now scornfully surrounded with thorns, Thine only crown;
O sacred Head, what glory, what bliss till now was Thine!
Yet, though despised and gory, I joy to call Thee mine.

What Thou, my Lord, hast suffered, was all for sinners' gain;
Mine, mine was the transgression, but Thine the deadly pain.
Lo, here I fall, my Savior! 'Tis I deserve Thy place;
Look on me with Thy favor, vouchsafe to me Thy grace.

Men mock and taunt and jeer Thee, Thou noble countenance,
Though mighty worlds shall fear Thee and flee before Thy
glance.
How art thou pale with anguish, with sore abuse and scorn!
How doth Thy visage languish that once was bright as morn!

Now from Thy cheeks has vanished their color once so fair;
From Thy red lips is banished the splendor that was there.
Grim death, with cruel rigor, hath robbed Thee of Thy life;
Thus Thou hast lost Thy vigor, Thy strength in this sad strife.

My burden in Thy Passion, Lord, Thou hast borne for me,
For it was my transgression which brought this woe on Thee.
I cast me down before Thee, wrath were my rightful lot;
Have mercy, I implore Thee; Redeemer, spurn me not!

What language shall I borrow to thank Thee, dearest friend,
For this Thy dying sorrow, Thy pity without end?
O make me Thine forever, and should I fainting be,
Lord, let me never, never outlive my love to Thee.

My Shepherd, now receive me; my Guardian, own me Thine.
Great blessings Thou didst give me, O source of gifts divine.
Thy lips have often fed me with words of truth and love;
Thy Spirit oft hath led me to heavenly joys above.

Here I will stand beside Thee, from Thee I will not part;
O Savior, do not chide me! When breaks Thy loving heart,
When soul and body languish in death's cold, cruel grasp,
Then, in Thy deepest anguish, Thee in mine arms I'll clasp.

The joy can never be spoken, above all joys beside,
When in Thy body broken I thus with safety hide.
O Lord of Life, desiring Thy glory now to see,
Beside Thy cross expiring, I'd breathe my soul to Thee.

My Savior, be Thou near me when death is at my door;
Then let Thy presence cheer me, forsake me nevermore!
When soul and body languish, oh, leave me not alone,
But take away mine anguish by virtue of Thine own!

Be Thou my consolation, my shield when I must die;
Remind me of Thy passion when my last hour draws nigh.
Mine eyes shall then behold Thee, upon Thy cross shall dwell,
My heart by faith enfolds Thee. Who dieth thus dies well.

Day 40: Saturday

<hr style="border:none; text-align:center;">
❧

Holy Saturday

Read: John 19: 38-42

Joseph of Arimathea asked Pilate for the body of Jesus last night, knowing the bodies would be off the cross before the Sabbath. With his permission, he came and took Jesus to a tomb that had never been used. Before placing him there, another disciple Nicodemus brought along a mixture of 75 pounds of myrrh and aloes. The two men took Jesus' body and wrapped it with the spices and placed him in and among clean strips of linen. They placed Jesus in the tomb. There his body lay, in a solitary cave with a large stone covering the doorway. Guarded well. Sealed. Protected. Alone.

After the upheaval of the previous day, the shared grief of watching Jesus suffer and die, today is left for quiet mourning and reflection. How had the outstretched arms of love led Jesus to such a lonely place?

We wonder the same ourselves, now two millennia later. The Jesus we watched grows from the infant miraculously born to the virgin, under the watchful tutelage of his carpenter father, and among his siblings in a crude home in Nazareth. His wisdom and stature and favor with God and man expanded exponentially over the years until he was baptized, tested, blessed and sent out to fulfill his mission.

We noted with the gospel writers his calling of the disciples to cease being fishermen to become instead fishers of men. We watched with awe his miraculous turning of water into wine, making right that which was wrong, healing hurting bodies and troubled souls, welcoming children and strangers, teaching in parables, and ushering in the Kingdom of heaven. We learned from his example of caring for the suffering, advocating for the weak, encouraging the broken-hearted, and restoring blind eyes, closed ears, and forgotten souls. We listened intently to his every word, and our lives are forever changed.

And now we walk with Joseph and Nicodemus to the tomb. And we wait and watch with those who are stunned and doubting, and yet hoping and praying for a miracle. It's the day after we saw Jesus die so miserably on the cross. We can hardly get the sights out of our minds eye, the smell out of our nostrils, the sadness out of our hearts. It was horrible to stand by helplessly as the victim of such cruelty was our friend, our teacher, our mentor, our guide. We trusted him, walked with him, and now we mourn.

Is it all going to end in this tragic way? We're no longer all together. We're stunned and saddened. We're not sure what's next. We hope. We pray. We linger. We trust. We rest. We wait.

Behold Jesus in our memories and now in the tomb; believe in the words he once spoke as truth; belong to the ones who hold fast to his promises; and become a member of the family of Jesus who forever sing his praise as the One who came to life miraculously and will rise again miraculously once more. Amen.

———∽∾∽———

For additional reflection today, prayerfully consider the words of this ancient Holy Week hymn, "Were You There?" written by African-American slaves in the late 19th Century:

Were you there when they crucified my Lord?
Were you there when they crucified my Lord?
Oh, sometimes it causes me to tremble, tremble, tremble.
Were you there when they crucified my Lord?

Were you there when they nailed him to the tree?
Were you there when they nailed him to the tree?
Oh, sometimes it causes me to tremble, tremble, tremble.
Were you there when they nailed him to the tree?

Outstretched Arms of Grace

Were you there when they laid him in the tomb?
Were you there when they laid him in the tomb?
Oh, sometimes it causes me to tremble, tremble, tremble.
Were you there when they laid him in the tomb?

Were you there when God raised him from the tomb?
Were you there when God raised him from the tomb?
Oh, sometimes it causes me to tremble, tremble, tremble.
Were you there when God raised him from the tomb?

Resurrection Sunday

❧

Easter Sunday

Read: Matthew 28: 1-10; John 20: 1-9 (in addition to Easter Scripture readings below)

Behold him risen and reigning forever – Alleluia! Believe in the Gospel of Christ and be set free to love and worship him as forgiven, restored, and redeemed! Belong to the Church triumphant who will live together with Christ for all eternity! Become a new creature in Christ Jesus, who experiences breaking in your making, rising from your falling, and living from your dying – both now and forevermore!

For your prayerful reflection today, consider the words of this ancient Easter hymn, "Christ the Lord Is Risen Today, Alleluia!" written by Charles and John Wesley in 1739:

Christ the Lord is ris'n today, Alleluia!
Sons of men and angels say, Alleluia!
Raise your joys and triumphs high, Alleluia!
Sing, ye heav'ns, and earth, reply, Alleluia!

Lives again our glorious King, Alleluia!
Where, O death, is now thy sting? Alleluia!
Once He died our souls to save, Alleluia!
Where thy victory, O grave? Alleluia!

Love's redeeming work is done, Alleluia!
Fought the fight, the battle won, Alleluia!
Death in vain forbids His rise, Alleluia!
Christ hath opened paradise, Alleluia!

Soar we now where Christ hath led, Alleluia!
Foll'wing our exalted Head, Alleluia!
Made like Him, like Him we rise, Alleluia!
Ours the cross, the grave, the skies, Alleluia!

Hail the Lord of earth and heaven, Alleluia!
Praise to Thee by both be given, Alleluia!
Thee we greet triumphant now, Alleluia!
Hail the Resurrection, thou, Alleluia!

King of glory, Soul of bliss, Alleluia!
Everlasting life is this, Alleluia!
Thee to know, Thy pow'r to prove, Alleluia!
Thus to sing, and thus to love, Alleluia!

Easter Monday and Beyond

❧

Outstretched Arms of Grace Continues On!

Read: Luke 24: 13-35

Behold him living in and through his beloved children all along life's journeys! Believe that he will continue to appear to you in the releasing of the Word and in fellowship with his Spirit! Belong to the ones who discern when their hearts are burning with every sense of his presence and peace! Become a beloved child of the Triune God who anticipates new life in Jesus with each new day!

⸻

For your prayerful reflection today, consider the words of this ancient Holy Week hymn, "I Cannot Tell…" by William Fullerton, 1929:

I cannot tell why He whom angels worship,
Should set His love upon the sons of men,
Or why, as shepherd, He should seek the wanderers,
To bring them back, they know not how or when.
But this I know, that He was born of Mary
When Bethlehem's manger was His only home,
And that He lived at Nazareth and labored,
And so the Savior, Savior of the world is come.

I cannot tell how silently He suffered,
As with His peace He graced this place of tears,
Or how His heart upon the cross was broken,
The crown of pain to three and thirty years.
But this I know, He heals the brokenhearted,
And stays our sin, and calms our lurking fear,
And lifts the burden from the heavy laden,
For yet the Savior, Savior of the world is here.

I cannot tell how He will win the nations,
How He will claim His earthly heritage,
How satisfy the needs and aspirations
Of East and West, of sinner and of sage.
But this I know, all flesh shall see His glory,
And He shall reap the harvest He has sown,
And some glad day His sun shall shine in splendor
When He the Savior, Savior of the world is known.

I cannot tell how all the lands shall worship,
When, at His bidding, every storm is stilled,

Or who can say how great the jubilation
When all the hearts of men with love are filled.
But this I know, the skies will thrill with rapture,
And myriad, myriad human voices sing,
And earth to Heaven, and Heaven to earth, will answer:
At last the Savior, Savior of the world is king!

About the Author

Stephen A. Macchia is the Founder and President of Leadership Transformations, Inc. (LTI), a ministry focusing on the spiritual formation needs of leaders and the spiritual discernment processes of leadership teams in local church and parachurch ministry settings. In conjunction with his leadership of LTI, he also serves as the director of the Pierce Center for Disciple-Building at Gordon-Conwell Theological Seminary. He is the author of several books, including *Becoming a Healthy Church*, *Becoming a Healthy Disciple*, *Becoming A Healthy Team*, *Crafting A Rule of Life*, and *Broken and Whole*. Stephen and his wife, Ruth, are the proud parents of Nathan and Rebekah and reside in Lexington, Massachusetts.

For more information about Stephen A. Macchia or Leadership Transformations, Inc., visit:

www.LeadershipTransformations.org
www.HealthyChurch.net
www.RuleOfLife.com

Other Titles by Stephen A. Macchia

In **Broken and Whole** Stephen A. Macchia offers the gifts of love found in 1 Corinthians 13 as the antidote to our brokenness. He writes with personal transparency from his own experience. Each chapter concludes with a powerful spiritual assessment tool to use in reflecting on our own leadership strengths and weaknesses. By embracing and befriending our own brokenness we can find true wholeness in God's strength. As you progress through the book, you will discover a new way to live in freedom and joy.

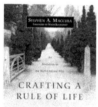

In **Crafting a Rule of Life** Stephen A. Macchia looks to St. Benedict as a guide for discovering your own rule of life in community. It is a process that takes time and concerted effort; you must listen to God and discern what he wants you to be and do for his glory. But through the basic disciplines of Scripture, prayer and reflection in a small group context this practical workbook will lead you forward in a journey toward Christlikeness.

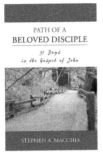

Welcome to the delightful journey of discipleship! Jesus invites us to say an enthusiastic "Yes!" to his beckoning call: Come close, draw near, and follow me. This is exactly what John the Beloved Disciple said long ago and it's our invitation to intimacy today. Becoming a "beloved disciple" of Jesus is the focus of the 31 reflections contained in this devotional guide.

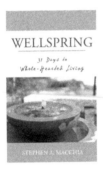

The Bible is filled with more than 50 different depictions of the heart, such as hardened, humble, deceitful and grateful. God's desire is to woo his followers to devote their whole heart to him in all aspects of their personal life and worship: loving God with "all" their heart...as well as with their soul, mind, and strength.

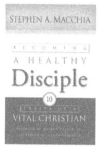

Becoming a Healthy Disciple explores the ten traits of a healthy disciple, including a vital prayer life, evangelistic outreach, worship, servanthood, and stewardship. He applies to individual Christians the ten characteristics of a healthy church outlined in his previous book, *Becoming a Healthy Church*. Discipleship is a lifelong apprenticeship to Jesus Christ, the master teacher. Macchia looks to John the beloved disciple as an example of a life lived close to Christ.

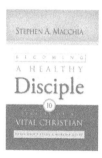

Becoming a Healthy Disciple Small Group Study & Worship Guide is a companion to Steve Macchia's book, *Becoming a Healthy Disciple*. This small group guide provides discussion and worship outlines to enrich your study of the ten traits of a healthy disciple. This 12-week small group resource provides Study, Worship, and Prayer guidelines for each session.

Becoming a Healthy Team is essential for building the kingdom. Stephen A. Macchia offers tried and tested principles and practices to help your leadership team do the same. He'll show you how to Trust, Empower, Assimilate, Manage, and Serve. That spells TEAMS and ultimately success. Filled with scriptural guideposts, *Becoming a Healthy Team* provides practical answers and pointed questions to keep your team on track and moving ahead.

In **Becoming a Healthy Church**, Stephen A. Macchia illustrates how to move beyond church growth to church health. Healthy growth is a process that requires risk taking, lifestyle changes, and ongoing evaluation. This book is a practical, hands-on manual to launch you and your church into a process of positive change. Available in 4 Languages: English, Chinese, Korean, Spanish.

Additional Resouces @
SPIRITUALFORMATIONSTORE.COM

Guide to Prayer for All Who Walk With God

The latest from Rueben Job, A Guide to Prayer for All Who Walk With God offers a simple pattern of daily prayer built around weekly themes and organized by the Christian church year. Each week features readings for reflection from such well-known spiritual writers as Francis of Assisi, Teresa of Avila, Dietrich Bonhoeffer, Henri J. M. Nouwen, Sue Monk Kidd, Martin Luther, Julian of Norwich, M. Basil Pennington, Evelyn Underhill, Douglas Steere, and many others.

Guide to Prayer for All Who Seek God

For nearly 20 years, people have turned to the Guide to Prayer series for a daily rhythm of devotion and personal worship. Thousands of readers appreciate the series' simple structure of daily worship, rich spiritual writings, lectionary guidelines, and poignant prayers. Like its predecessors,

A Guide to Prayer for All Who Seek God will become a treasured favorite for those hungering for God as the Christian year unfolds.

Guide to Prayer for Ministers and Other Servants

A best-seller for more than a decade! This classic devotional and prayer book includes thematically arranged material for each week of the year as well as themes and schedules for 12 personal retreats. The authors have adopted the following daily format for this prayer book: daily invocations, readings, scripture, reflection, prayers, weekly hymns, benedictions, and printed psalms.

Guide to Prayer for All God's People

A compilation of scripture, prayers and spiritual readings, this inexhaustible resource contains thematically arranged material for each week of the year and for monthly personal retreats. Its contents have made it a sought-after desk reference, a valuable library resource and a cherished companion.

LEADERSHIP
TRANSFORMATIONS <u>INC.</u>
FORMATION | DISCERNMENT | RENEWAL

- Soul Care Retreats and Soul Sabbaths
- Emmaus: Spiritual Leadership Communities
- Selah: Certificate Program in Spiritual Direction (Selah-West, Selah-East)
- Spiritual Formation Groups
- Spiritual Health Assessments
- Spiritual Discernment for Teams
- Sabbatical Planning
- Spiritual Formation Resources

Visit www.LeadershipTransformations.org or call (877) TEAM LTI.